THE CHAMPIONSHIPS
WIMBLEDON
Official Annual 2004

Neil Harman

Photographs By: Clive Brunskill, Mike Hewitt, Phil Cole, Clive Rose, and Scott Barbour of Getty Images

Publisher
EDDIE TAYLOR

Publicity and promotion
LAURA FELL

Art Editor
STEVE SMALL

Photography
CLIVE BRUNSKILL
MIKE HEWITT
PHIL COLE
CLIVE ROSE
SCOTT BARBOUR

Photo research, Getty Images
ELAINE LOBO

Photographs copyright © 2004 Getty Images

This first edition published in 2004 by Hazleton Publishing Ltd,
5th Floor Mermaid House, 2 Puddle Dock, London EC4V 3DS

Hazleton Publishing Ltd is part of
Profile Media Group Plc

ISBN: 1-903135 39 7

Printed by

Mondadori

Colour Reproduction by:

Wyndeham Graphics Kent

www.wyndeham-graphics.co.uk

Results tables are reproduced by courtesy of
The All England Lawn Tennis Club

This book is reproduced with the assistance of Rolex

ROLEX

FOREWORD

THE 118th Championships will be remembered for the wonderful singles finals after earlier rain delays had tested the nerve of the players and the patience of everyone else.

The men's singles final saw the two top-ranked players in the world fighting for the title. Andy Roddick "threw the kitchen sink" at defending champion Roger Federer and, as he added ruefully afterwards, "received a bathtub back". It was a compelling contest with Roddick pushing Federer to the limit of his quite exceptional ability before the Swiss top seed finally won out in the fourth set.

While Roger Federer remained King of Wimbledon, 17 year-old Maria Sharapova became the new Princess, winning both the ladies' singles Championship and international adulation. The 13th-seeded Russian (five other Russians were seeded above her, indicating that Russia has become a major force in world tennis) beat former Wimbledon champion Lindsay Davenport in three exciting sets in the semi-final before sensationally dethroning defending champion Serena Williams in a dramatic final. Maria Sharapova, having won the first set, was 2-4 down

in the second when she launched an extraordinary display of uninhibited hitting, leavened with two wonderful attacking lobs, to end the run of Williams wins in the ladies' singles – Venus and Serena had won two titles each in the preceding four years.

Todd Woodbridge set an all-time Wimbledon record in the men's doubles by winning his ninth men's doubles title and his third in succession with Jonas Bjorkman. And Cara Black achieved a double in winning the ladies' doubles with Rennae Stubbs and the mixed doubles with her brother Wayne.

All in all, the players served up a great deal of memorable tennis which deserved much better weather. I hope you enjoy this record of Wimbledon 2004.

Tim Phillips

Tim Phillips
Chairman of The All England Lawn Tennis & Croquet Club
and the Committee of Management of The Championships

ORDER
OF
PLAY
SUNDAY 27th JUNE
2004

Main photo: The uncertain weather
meant that the covers were much in
evidence during the tournament.

Left: clockwise from top left: An extra
day had to be scheduled on the middle
Sunday; Henman had his usual colouful
support; In safe hands, Federer
retained his Men's title; A shining new
star emerged in the Women's game in
the form of Sharapova.

Right: John Parsons.

INTRODUCTION

JOHN PARSONS, the lawn tennis correspondent of the *Daily Telegraph*, had been author of this illustrious account of the Wimbledon championships since its inception in 1983 – this would have been his 22nd consecutive annual – a labour of love for which he gave his all. There was a distinct pall hanging over the All England Club the day before The 2004 Championships and it had nothing to do with sheets of rain scudding through SW19.

Parsons, or JP, as he was affectionately known, had passed away in Miami, Florida in April, having suffered complications from kidney failure. The entire tennis-writing world mourned a man whose love for his sport transcended most everything else in his life.

St Mary's, the church that overlooks the grounds, was packed to the rafters for John's memorial service on Sunday, June 20th. All of his friends were there – his parents, too, both in their nineties – and Tim Henman, the Great Britain No.1 who hails from Oxfordshire, John's county, and whose career had been chronicled with an abiding sense of warmth and affection ever since their paths first crossed. Henman, in immaculate suit and club tie, read a stirring passage from St John's Gospel that opened with the words: "Let not your hearts be troubled; believe in God, believe also in me." The choice was apposite.

There is nothing more that John Parsons would have desired than for Tim Henman to become the Wimbledon champion one day, to lay the ghost of however many years it was now since Fred Perry had lifted the coveted gold trophy. Henman's march into the semi-finals of the French Open at Roland Garros stirred the cauldron of expectation more than ever, and even though he lost his first match in the Stella Artois championship at Queen's and chose not to play another tour match in the meantime, the frenzy was all too familiar.

Could Henman do it? The draw looked decent enough, but that was a battle fought on paper with no regard for any man's approach, fitness and quality on any given day. Many a player had won a title when the draw was made. Assumption was fine, but it was no more than that. JP always preferred to deal in facts.

There were a couple of players who looked in exceedingly decent touch, not least the defending champion Roger Federer from Switzerland, whose breakthrough in grand slam events the previous year had inspired him to previously uncharted heights. He was victorious in the Masters Cup in Houston – where the eight best players in the world over a calendar year faced off – and the Australian Open in January, which he won with considerable aplomb. Andy Roddick, the No.2 seed, had won at Queen's for the second consecutive year and, in doing so, had broken the service speed record, clocking up 153mph. This really was nothing like the tennis JP had known at the start of his career when wooden rackets prevailed and the thought of a speed gun on court was the stuff of sci-fi fantasy.

The women's section had lost its two main attractions, the No.1 and No.2 players in the world, Justine Henin-Hardenne and Kim Clijsters, both from Belgium (though Clijsters was there to urge on her fiancé, Lleyton Hewitt). Henin-Hardenne, the 2001 runner up, had not recovered from a viral infection that had been troubling her since March; Clijsters' left wrist was so heavily strapped that she could not even applaud Hewitt's finer strokes.

But the Williams sisters, one or either of whom had won the previous four finals, were restored to the sport after months of interruption through injury or other engagements. Though they had slipped down the WTA ranking list, a complex arrangement involving past form and results against individual fellow competitors, meant that Serena would be seeded No.1 and Venus No.3. What was more, the draw kept them apart, raising the promise of a third consecutive final meeting between the two.

The LTA's wild card play-off had offered Arvind Parmar, newly installed as British No.2 ahead of Greg Rusedski, Mark Hilton and Richard Bloomfield a place in the draw; but rather than offer Ian Flanagan, who had defeated Mark Philippoussis and Victor Hanescu at Queen's similar treatment, the committee decided the final wild card should go to Todd Reid of Australia, a former boy's singles champion.

Of the eight women granted wild cards, the most controversial was that given to the 47-year-old Martina Navratilova, a nine-time singles champion who stood one title away from beating Billie Jean King's Wimbledon record of 20. Navratilova said she was only playing singles to enhance her doubles prospects and yet she was given a wild card, a decision that led to several raised eyebrows.

Whatever the rights and wrongs, the whys and wherefores, there was the usual sense of adrenaline rush as we walked down Church Road to prepare for the flag to go down. We knew the next 13 days would bring unremitting courage and colour, despair and delirium, magnificence and moonbeams. We sorely missed JP, but on this day he revered among all others, we could not wait.

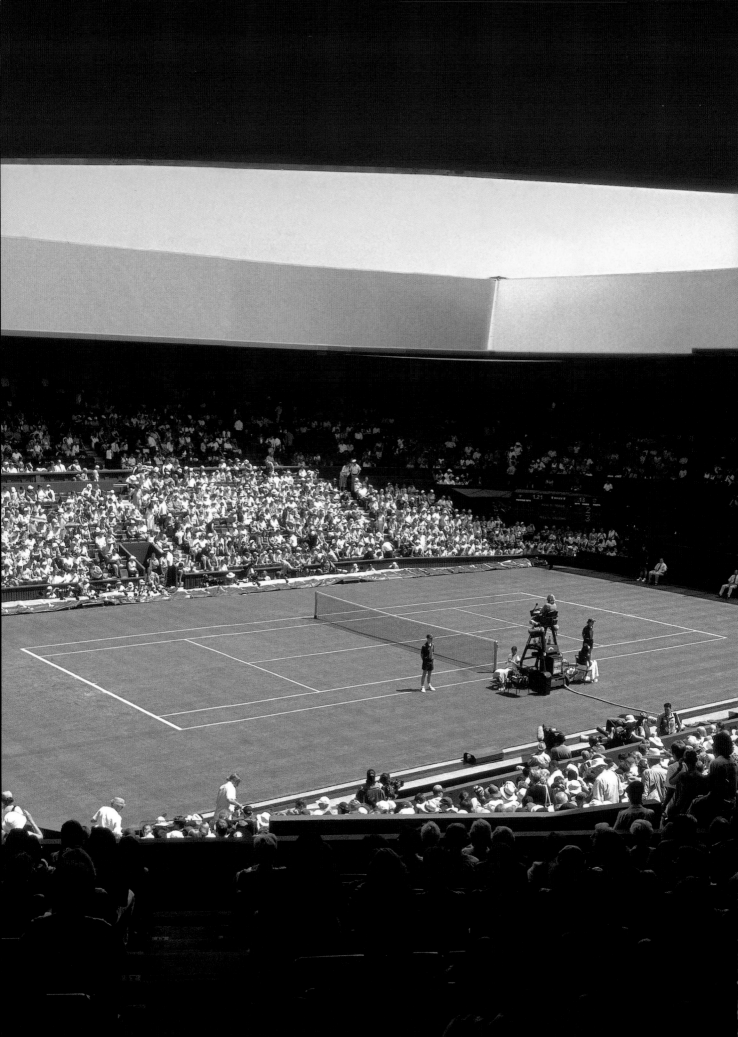

THERE IS A MOMENT WHEN YOU BECOME

PART OF TIME.

AND A MOMENT WHEN YOU BECOME

PART OF HISTORY.

There is only one Wimbledon. And in the minds of those who play and dream of winning, there is only one Centre Court. It's the place where legends come of age and, on occasion, hearts are broken. For 25 years we have respected the traditions of Wimbledon and admired their timeless beauty. After all, those who rule at Wimbledon have seized their moment and their achievements are indelibly written in time. **THE WIMBLEDON CHAMPIONSHIPS – JUNE 21ST TO JULY 4TH, 2004.**

OYSTER PERPETUAL DAY-DATE · WWW.ROLEX.COM

ROLEX

Roger Federer (SWZ).

Age: 22.

Born: Basel, Switzerland.

His 2003 triumph at the Championships triggered a remarkable sequence of successes for the all-court technician who had slipped so easily into the role as the world No.1. He went on to win the Masters Cup in Houston and lift the Australian Open title in Melbourne, highlights in his plundering of tournament after tournament in the build up to the defence of his title. Indeed, he had not lost on grass since the first round of Wimbledon in 2002, when he had been beaten by Mario Ancic. Federer had also taken the controversial decision to work on his own, having parted company with Peter Lundgren, his coach, at Christmas. It was going to need a severe dip in his form or a huge rise in someone else for anyone to stop him.

1

THE CHAMPIONSHIPS • MEN'S SEEDS

Andy Roddick (USA).

Age: 21.

Born: Omaha, USA.

Having won back-to-back Stella Artois titles at the Queen's Club, there was no doubting the American's enhanced grass court pedigree. Roddick finished 2003 as the official No.1 ranked player in the world after his stunning period of success on the hard courts of his homeland, two Masters Series victories and finally the US Open, his first major. With his serve, that had just topped off at a record-breaking 153mph, and improved quality off the ground, Roddick was in tune and a year into his partnership with Brad Gilbert, seemed more capable than ever.

2

Guillermo Coria (Arg).

Age: 21.

Born: Rufino, Argentina.

Guillermo had lost in the first round on his previous two visits to the Championships and was coming off a disheartening loss in the final of the French Open to Gaston Gaudio, his compatriot. Then, after suffering a severe bout of cramp when in total control of the match, Coria fought back to have two match points but could not convert them. He had said that to be consiered a champion you had to win on all surfaces and was willing to give the Championships his best shot. Regarded as the quickest man on tour, with tremendous staying power, Coria had just begun to work with Gabriel Markus, who inspired David Nalbandian to the 2002 final.

Tim Henman (GB).

Age: 29.

Born: Oxford, England.

It had all been said many times over, but this year there was a subtle twist. Henman had been Britiain's finest hope of a home victory for over 60 years and continued to wow his audiences, but since last year's Championships, he had won his first Masters Series at the Paris Indoors, begun working with Paul Annacone, formerly coach to Pete Sampras, and reached the semi-finals of the French Open, where he led Guillermo Coria by a set and a break of serve. An opening round defeat at Queen's Club was regarded as a minor blip; Henman was still the most natural grass court player in the field.

6

Juan Carlos Ferrero (SP).

Age: 23.

Born: Onteniente, Spain.

The 2003 French Open champion had endured an up-and-down 12 months. Building on that triumph by reaching the final of the US Open, Ferrero then won the Madrid Masters, and played in the Davis Cup Final in Melbourne. He then reached the semi-finals of the Australian Open and the final in Rotterdam, before he was debilitated by a bout of chickenpox, weakening him at the onset of the clay court season. He never really got going in the spring and was beaten in the third round of the French this year by Igor Andreev, an unheralded Russian. Ferrero decided to go home to Barcelona and practice on a grass court rather than play any of the lead-up events.

Lleyton Hewitt (Aus).

Age: 23.

Born: Adelaide, Australia.

There were definite signs of a possible rennaisance in the form of the 2002 champion. Having chosen to miss the latter part of last year to prepare for the Davis Cup Final – a successful decision given Australia's victory over Spain – Hewitt won Sydney in the first two weeks of the year and played brilliantly to defeat Ferrero in the Rotterdam final. His clay court form was patchy until reaching the semi-finals in Hamburg and a quarter-final at Roland Garros. Defeated in the semi-final of the Stella Artois championships, Hewitt was nevertheless playing and speaking with an increasing assurance.

7

8

Rainer Schuettler (Ger).

Age: 28.

Born: Korbach, Germany.

It had been a wondrous 2003 for the German who broke the bonds of that awful word 'journeyman'. He completed his best professional season by finishing in the top ten (at No.6 no less) for the first time in his career, which improved his year-on-year ranking for the ninth straight time. Having reached back-to-back Masters Series semi-finals in the later summer, Schuettler also secured a place in the semi-finals of the Masters Cup in Houston, losing to Andre Agassi from a set up. He lost a series of first round matches at the start of 2004 but was recovering a semblance of form and is regarded as the fittest player on the tour.

Carlos Moya (SP).

Age: 27.

Born: Palma de Mallorca, Spain.

Moya missed the past two Wimbledons, preferring to rest after the endurance period of the clay court season. But he had a change of heart and was determined to do well at the 2004 Championships and prepared by playing in an exhibition at Stoke Poges. Possessing possibly the most fearsome forehand in the game – remarkable considering he is actually left handed – the 1998 French Open champion had started to look as if he was striking excellent form, as seven of his 14 career titles had come in the past two years indicated.

9

1

Serena Williams (USA).

Age: 22.

Born: Saginaw, USA.

With no Justine Henin-Hardenne and no Kim Clijsters, the top two players in the world, Serena Williams was a favoured choice to win her third consecutive title on the Wimbledon lawns. What counted against the defending champion was her lack of truly competitive matches at the highest level. After an eight-month period of recuperation from an operation on her knee and the diversion of a budding career as an actress, no one could quite be certain what levels of desire Serena still possessed. A fourth round defeat to Jennifer Capriati at the French Open suggested she was a decent way short of being the champion of old.

THE CHAMPIONSHIPS • WOMEN'S SEEDS

Anastasia Myskina (Russia).

Age: 23.

Born: Moscow, Russia.

Burst onto the scene in emphatic style at Roland Garros, carrying all before her, to defeat compatriot Elena Dementieva and win her first grand slam. Seven years previously, Myskina reached her first-ever tour final in the ITF-event at Batumi in the former Soviet republic of Georgia. Then, as No.762 in the world, Myskina defeated the No.514, who just happened to be Dementieva. Myskina's progress through the rankings had been solid, though nothing prepared the world for her success in Paris, where she saved a match point in the fourth round against Svetlana Kuznetsova before defeating Dementieva 6-1, 6-2 in 59 minutes, the fastest final there for 16 years. She had become the first Russian woman to reach the final of a slam since Olga Morozova in 1974.

3

2 Venus Williams (USA).

Age: 24.

Born: Lynwood, USA.

Given special dispensation for a huge rise from her ranking of 11 to a seeded position of No.3, the draw did, at least, prevent the prospect of a third successive Williams final – and the seventh overall in grand slams – the interest in which had become increasingly difficult to sustain. She had lost in her past four major finals, all to her sister, and was beaten at the French Open a month earlier on the same day as Serena. The fact that such reverses had ceased to be a huge surprise led to debate about the depth of her desire. However, she was twice a former Wimbledon champion and though she had been troubled with injuries for the past few months – most notably a recurring stomach muscle problem – she seemed relaxed and at ease in the build up.

Amelie Mauresmo (France).

Age: 25

Born: St Germain en Laye, France.

The consummate all court player - the 1999 Australian Open runner up and twice a semi-finalist at Wimbledon and the US Open last year. The only reason she had not become a grand slam champion was a career-long tendency to become consumed by nerves on the big occasions. That had certainly happened in France – even after winning the titles in Rome and Berlin – and she talked openly in the build up to Wimbledon about it being somewhere she could get away from the scrutiny that devoured her at home. Played Eastbourne for the first time where she reached the semi-finals, and believes that in partnership with coach Loic Courteau, she will eventually break her duck.

5

Lindsay Davenport (USA).

Age: 28.

Born: Palos Verdes, California.

The 1999 champion had won her 40th career title – and topped £10 million in prize money, becoming only the fourth lady in history to achieve that milestone – at Amelia Island in April. This demonstrated that she still has enough life and drive in her to challenge the big names. A quarter-final at the Australian Open and fourth round at the French were, however, indicators of a less than formidable presence at the grand slams than she used to be. However, she remains one of the cleanest strikers of the tennis ball and if she were to get on a roll, could be very difficult to stop.

Elena Dementieva (Rus).

Age: 22

Born: Moscow, Russia.

Another of the fast-rising Russians. Dementieva reached the semi-finals of the US Open in 2000, but had not really built on that in the grand slams until an immense break through at the French Open where she reached the final – defeating Amelie Mauresmo on the way to intense French disappointment. Her mother, Vera, had been a constant companion through her formative professional years. However, since the start of 2004, Dementieva had starting working with Olga Morozova, the most famed of past Russian players, and was showing encouraging signs of progress. Her serve did, though, have a tendency to break down when under the severest pressure.

6

7

Jennifer Capriati (USA).

Age: 28.

Born: New York City, USA.

Though Jennifer had twice won the Australian Open and once at the French, the two titles she most wanted, the US Open and Wimbledon, had continued to elude her. At Flushing Meadows in 2003, she was involved in one of the all-time most memorable matches, losing in a final set tie-break to Justine Henin-Hardenne who promptly had to be placed on an intravenous drip. She is best remembered as a 15-year-old in 1990 giving Martina Navratilova, the defending champion, her earliest defeat at the Championships since the year Capriati was born.

Svetlana Kuznetsova (Rus).

Age: 19.

Born: St Petersburg, Russia.

The Russians had never been more prominently placed in the Wimbledon seedings. The teenage Kuznetsova, who had begun the year ranked No.35, had made enormous strides, in both singles, where she had advanced into the top 20 by March, and doubles, including an appearance in the final of the Australian Open with Elena Likhovtseva. She had also shared the enviable experience of playing several tournaments with Martina Navratilova. Kuznetsova came into the Championships having won the Hastings Direct title at Eastbourne on its eve, was at a career-high No.9 and had reached the quarter-finals last year, so was highly effective on grass.

8

Crowds gather around the
Fred Perry statue and pray
for a break in the clouds.

Inclement weather
conditions have
delayed play

Day 1 · Federer v Bogdanovic

THERE have been so many glittering moments in the rich, varied tapestry of Wimbledon that are of cherished value – an extended flick through the finest compendium in the world of tennis would confirm that – it is difficult to know where to start. Even on Day One. But the thought of two of the sport's contemporary finest lighting up the first day of The 118th Championships meant that those who had managed to lay their hands on tickets for Monday, June 21st – and seen that the weather had designs on being kind – were among the most fortunate All England Club visitors in recent memory.

The traditional time for the defending men's champion to take his place, opening afternoon on Centre Court, became the time for two such notables to share the limelight. Roger Federer, by dint of his 2003 victory, would have first use of the Centre Court but, in his wake, would come Goran Ivanisevic, the magical man from Croatia, who had not been back to Wimbledon – through sheer freakish misfortune – since leaving it wreathed in glory in 2001.

Federer was playing British wild card Alex Bogdanovic in a match behind which there was a fascinating sub-plot. Bogdanovic, of Yugoslav extraction, had made his Davis Cup debut for Great Britain against Australia (facing no less an opponent than Lleyton Hewitt) 18 months earlier, but had subsequently been unable to live up to that promise. As such, the Lawn Tennis Association had decided to withdraw funding and drop him from their squads for a trial period, to see if it might buck his ideas up. What better way for the just-turned 20 year-old to respond to his "punishment" than give the defending champion a hard time on what was bound to be a nervous moment for him?

Intriguingly, when Ivanisevic was ruled out of returning to Wimbledon in 2002, the committee asked Hewitt, then world No.1, if he would like to begin proceedings. The Australian said he would rather not because he believed the grass would be too pure, too swift, a mite too glassy, for his liking. Hewitt, spared such a trial, won the title. A year later, when tradition dictated he must be first onto

Above: Security at The Championships was handled with admirable efficiency.
Left: Reigning champion, Roger Federer.
Below: Young British pretender, Alex Bogdanovic.

did two years ago when I lost in the first round [to Croatia's Mario Ancic]. I told myself I was playing well from the baseline and didn't have to exaggerate by coming too much to the net."

Karlovic had obviously decided he rather enjoyed first day heroics and if Paradorn Srichaphan had felt that winning the Nottingham Open the week immediately preceding the championship would offer him protection for a while, he was to be sadly disappointed.

"When I saw the draw, I said 'Oh no',," explained Srichaphan. I knew it wouldn't be a long, long match but I had no rhythm to hit the ball." The ninth seed from Thailand held sway in the opening set but Karlovic began to boom down his serves from 6'10" – plus

Above: The giant Croat Ivo Karlovic unleashes another towering serve.
Right: Paradorn Srichapan stretches for a smash in his match against Karlovic.
Far right: Goran Ivanisevic saltues the Centre Court crowd after a first-round win in his last ever Championships.
Bottom right: Mikhail Youzhny takes aim at an Ivanisevic serve.

the stage, the Australian was defeated by Croatia's Ivo Karlovic.

So Federer had been given due warning. Better not underestimate the opposition; Bogdanovic's ranking of No.307 might mean nothing in the circumstances. It did take time for Federer to find his grass court feet and Bogdanovic began with bright intentions, but this was not a moment for slip-ups, no fanciful repeat of the previous year. Federer rightly prevailed 6-3, 6-3, 6-0. Bogdanovic could go back to his more personal battles.

"Once you're leading you can relax more," Federer said. "You can play either more consistent or you can actually go for more. That makes you feel good for the rest of the match. I didn't want to start serve-and-volleying on my first and second serve like I

Match of the day

Goran Ivanisevic v
Mikhail Youzhny

The sun was shining vividly and nostalgia took on a wondrous hue; Goran Ivanisevic was on the threshold of announcing an irreversible retirement, but had returned to the shrine of his greatest triumph and discovered that it has not finished with its blessings for him. Ivanisevic, given a thunderous ovation after a two year absence, lit up the Centre Court. He kissed the net, gave a thumbs up to the Almighty and, drinking in the emotion, kindled remembrances of one of the greatest of tennis glories which the crowd – between dashing for cover three times – simply marvelled at.

His 6-3, 7-6, 6-2 victory over Youzhny, the No.31 seed from Russia, was a staggering vindication of his desire to come back and give this event one last tilt. We hoped his valediction would last more than a single day and the 32-year-old, who won the title on a wild card three years ago, won through to the second round; if he woke without too many twinges, the closing chapter could make for some reading.

"This was beautiful, the first time in the first round on Centre Court in my career," he said. "The grass is so lovely. The last I played here I had a great memory. You can be nervous but you cannot play a bad match on this court. I had luck today but he [Youzhny] had no chance, luck or not luck. I really played so well today."

Above: Young Argentine Guillermo Coria.
Above centre: Swede Thomas Johansson.
Above right: Aussie battler Lleyton Hewitt strikes a familiar pose.
Right: American Robbie Ginepri.
Below: Jurgen Melzer from Austria.

Above: Jamie Delgado.
Right: Juan-Carlos Ferrero.
Over: Ivo Karlovic touches the sky.

reach – and secured a place in the second round with a 3-6, 6-4, 6-4, 6-4 victory.

Martina Navratilova wasn't used to winning matches 6-0, 6-1 even in her pomp – indeed it happened only four times in her Wimbledon career. The last time she managed it on these lawns was in the third round in 1993, when she defeated Patricia Hy-Boulais, when Navratilova was a sprightly 36 years of age. Now she played on an adjacent court to Amanda Janes, born five years after Navratilova's first appearance here. Then, Navratilova played Amanda's mother, Christine, in a Fred Perry shirt a couple of sizes too small, itched like crazy, and which she couldn't wait to take off afterwards and slip into something more comfortable.

Catalina Castano of Colombia, Navratilova's opponent, is ranked No.100 in the world, had lost 6-0, 6-0 in the first round of the Hastings Direct championship in Eastbourne a week earlier to Australia's Alicia Molik and, on her four previous appearances on grass, had not managed to win a set. At the time of the controversial award of a wild card, Navratilova was ranked No.1001, from where no player has won a singles match at Wimbledon, bar Barbara Schwartz in 2001, who had no ranking at all.

Give Navratilova her dues; hers was a classic cameo of its kind – serve and volley tennis in the manner that she, more than any other player in the modern era, has exemplified. Winning matches 6-0, 6-1 not only strengthens her case for a place in the party, but makes a mockery of the WTA's claim that women's tennis has an enviable strength in depth.

Shock of the day
British success

After the debacle of 2003, when not a single British woman was able to secure a place in the second round, the storyline this year was commendably different. Two of them, Anne Keothavong (right) and Emily Webley-Smith (above) stole the headlines with admirable wins. Particular credit must go to Keothavong, relishing her position as the British No.1 as she defeated veteran Australian Nicole Pratt for the loss of only four games.

Bristol's Webley-Smith, who was once coached for three months by 1987 Wimbledon champion Pat Cash, beat Severine Beltrame of France 7-6, 6-4, enjoying the finest moment of her career. It made up for the six-month sacrifice of 2003 when, after smashing her ankle playing tennis, she needed reconstructive surgery. "It's my first Wimbledon and it's fantastic just to be here," she said, "but I can't just enjoy that and not go out and compete on the court. That's what I'm here for." The next day it was to be the turn of Elena Baltacha and Jane O'Donoghue. Things were looking up.

Above: Venus Williams is stretched – for once.
Right: Amanda Janes wraps a running forehand down the line.
Below: Australian Amanda Stosur optimistically dons the shades for her first round match.

Top: Maria Sharapova shapes up to be the golden girl of Wimbledon fortnight.
Above: Lindsay Davenport hammers another two-hander into play.

Quote of the day

"It's not about age, it never should be. I think the message I would like to send, old or young, is just enjoy what you're doing, regardless of what it is. If you don't enjoy playing tennis, go and do something else. I give that message in speeches I'm asked to make to corporate executives. Do something that you love, that way you have no regrets."
Martina Navratilova

Williams, S v Zheng • Day 2

LADIES' Day and, for Serena Williams, a chance for redemption after what she had termed "my suicide in Paris." The quarter-final loss to Jennifer Capriati at Roland Garros had – as she probably expected – led to a rash of wildly uninformed stories about a fading interest that amounted to tennis obituaries. Was it the end of Serena, at 22? "I don't know why I did some the things I did there," she said. Behind that honest assertion lurked the grim determination of Williams that one bad day or one poor grand slam would not distract her from the bigger picture. This was no place for sad faces. This was Wimbledon and the arena always enlivened her life. "I don't get the feeling anywhere else that I get here," she said, mentioning that her relaxation before the championship included being glued to the Euro 2004 football finals. "I want to bend it like Beckham," she said, but not, we hoped, quite that far over the bar.

In front of the defending champion on Day One was the Chinese Ji Zheng, a veritable pocket dynamo, who was making a determined move in the rankings. Serena won 6-3, 6-1 and was rather taken aback that she should face criticism for the number of unforced errors in the match. "Feel free to come out on the practice court if you guys want to help out," she told the assembled throng after one question particularly offended her.

There was certainly not a lot that Miss Zheng could have done in the circumstances. Williams appeared to be moving pretty well, there was authority, there was panache, there was little by way of a threat to her. Serena's passage into the second round was complete.

There were smiles, too, from Daniela Hantuchova, who defeated Samantha Reeves of the USA 6-1, 6-4 and looked like she was enjoying herself on the court again after a miserable year. "I don't have to go into the details again," she said. "I'm focused on what's happening now."

Tears of joy were certainly in vogue for Elena Baltacha, the British player who had endured the agony of a liver illness that threatened her long-term participation in tennis. Baltacha, urged on by coaches Alan Jones and the former British No.1 Jo Durie, defeated Marta Marrero of Spain, 6-1, 6-3, playing with a quality that could scarcely have felt possible during her long, often painful recuperation. "My coaches say I'm some kind of walking miracle," Baltacha said.

Above: Ji Zheng chases down another Serena Williams (right) exocet.
Below left: British star Elena Baltacha's produces a massive return – in every sense.
Below: Daniela Hantuchova concentrates on the positives.

Celebrity of the day

Boris Yeltsin, former President of Russia

Mr Yelstin had been in the VIP box at the 2002 Davis Cup Final in Paris, next to Jacques Chirac, as Russia landed the Cup for the first time. Much to the alarm of his host and the security troupe, Yelstin then leap-frogged the front of the box and joined the team on court for the celebrations.

Someone obviously told him that was not the order of the day at Wimbledon, where a certain level of decorum is expected of all its guests. Yeltsin had an up-and-down day. The loss of Marat Safin, albeit to Dmitri Tursunov, a fellow Russian, was a blow. But the French Open champion, Anastasia Myskina, making her bow on Centre Court, duly won her first round match.

Yeltsin was always exuberant about tennis during his premiership, leaping about a court in white shorts and extolling the virtues of the game. And five years after Yeltsin stood down, that revolution finally seems to have produced a coup, if one played out on the other side of Europe in the courts of Wimbledon and Roland Garros.

Retired since 1999, Yeltsin, now 73, keeps a low profile in Russia; the one exception is his favourite sport. After Myskina, 22, carried off the French title earlier, Yeltsin took her out for lunch and regaled her with advice and criticism. "He is like a grandfather to us and lunch was really casual. He knows everything about tennis," Myskina enthused. "We discussed the matches and he was telling us how to play. He told me to play more shots down the line and improve my serve."

Ladies' Day • Day 2

Far left: France's Virginie Razzano contemplates the difficulties of grass.
Left: Patti Schnyder is all concentration on her way to defeating Akiko Morigami (below left).
Below: Britain's Jane O'Donohue.
Bottom right: Katie O'Brien, also of Britian, had to complete her French A-Level before her match with Maria Sanchez Lorenzo.

Henman v Hidalgo · Day 2

At that same time, on Court No.1, Tim Henman was enduring other agonies. For some reason, the court has never been one of his favourites and though Ruben Ramirez Hidalgo, a Spanish player as green as the grass itself, was expected to be a pushover, this was a grim experience for the British No.1. "Some good things can happen when you find a way to win," Henman said. It was the most optimistic element to come out of an afternoon of dark scudding clouds and deep foreboding.

Henman's 4-6, 7-6, 6-4, 6-2 victory turned on a backhand volley of beauty at 6-6 in the second set tie-break. It was a shot that only a player of rare gifts would attempt at such a big moment, a soft caress from the strings against a hugely powerful groundstroke, the ball dying on the other side of the net. The Spaniard, who had a couple of points to stretch his lead to two sets, watched it land and gave up the chase. He hadn't given up on the match but the wound was mortal.

The British No.1 wasn't exactly brilliant in either of the last two sets, and when he rolled off eight points in a row midway through the fourth they were passing the smelling salts around Henman Hill. Too many good shots had been followed by horrid ones for anything to be taken for granted, but he was still alive and if the texture of his performance had a subtle advantage, it is that it puts a dampener on the expectancy for a few days.

In the third game of the second set, Henman hit one second serve that almost struck his opponent on the shins first bounce. He was trailing 3-1, pegged Ramirez Hidalgo's serve for the first time for 3-3 but was still hanging on when we reached a tie-break. Henman's seventh double fault gave the Spaniard a 3-1 lead, and that he extended to 6-4 – resulting in two set points, the first of which was on his serve. Henman struck a perfect backhand return at his opponent's toes, forcing Ramirez Hidalgo into a backhand error. A service return struck long meant Henman was level and then, with No.1 Court in silent thrall, he played that exquisite volley.

And so was avoided a 27th defeat on grass that would have drawn a veil over the whole shooting match. Henman's distrust of No.1 court, with its slow surface, distance from the crowd and temperatures that always seem to be close to absolute zero even in the summer, has long been chronicled. He will hope that it is the first and last time he will have to appear there this year. The crucible beckoned. "I've been playing here for the past ten years and been in pretty tight matches," he said. "I'm sure the crowd are getting the hang of things by now. You only get one chance don't you? You've got to find a way. But I never felt the result was going to be in doubt." That was easy for him to say.

Opposite and below: Tim Henman in action during his first round match against Ruben Ramirez Hidalgo.
Bottom: Hidalgo plays his part in another Henman nail-biter.

Shock of the day

Dmitri Tursunov bt Marat Safin 4-6, 7-5, 6-3, 7-6.

Perhaps this was not the shock it seemed at the time. Marat Safin (below) had never been particularly comfortable on grass – his quarter-final in 2001 apart, he had only won twice at Wimbledon and had usually departed the grounds bemoaning anything he could think of. For a former grand slam champion, it was never an edifying sight.

But this time it was clear that Safin did not even want to be around, not least on the infamous Court No.2, where reputations had been savaged. The tousle-haired Tursunov (above), one of the up-and-coming youngsters on the circuit, was not put off by his compatriot's clear desire to be somewhere else. Even the presence of Boris Yeltsin, the former Russian president, could not coax the competitive sap from Safin. "I give up on Wimbledon, it is definitely not the tournament for me," Safin said. "I hate this, I have to admit it. I give up spending time on these courts. I'm not going to waste my time knowing that I'm not going to play well."

It was a particularly undignified departure from a player of such repute, one that demanded a closer inspection as it smacked of giving in.

Far left and left: Karel Kucera takes aim – and fires.
Above: Mardy Fish shows off his new ponytail.
Bottom left: Ivan Ljubicic of Croatia lost out to Grand Slam veteran Wayne Ferreira.
Centre: Young Australian Todd Reid in action against Vince Spadea.
Centre bottom: No stranger to the ponytail is Xavier Malisse, who defeated 16th seed Jiri Novak in straight sets.

Mens doubles: Leander Pees and David Rikl against Max Mirnyi and Mahesh Bhupathi

Game of the day
Tommy Haas v Antony Dupuis

It had been a long and difficult route back to this kind of arena for the German Tommy Haas; he's endured two bouts of shoulder surgery, and the very public suffering of an automobile accident in Florida that almost killed his father, Peter. He did not play at all in 2003 but was able to enter The Championships thanks to a protected ranking of No.11. When he lost the first two sets and took only four games against durable Frenchman, Antony Dupuis, all looked lost. But Haas slowly turned the match around, winning a memorable third set tie-break, 12-10 and holding it all together to win 2-6, 2-6, 7-6, 6-4, 8-6. Everyone hoped it would be the re-start of something really special for the likeable Haas.

WEDNESDAY 23 JUNE

Day 3

IT was the first full day's washout since Tuesday, June 29, 1999. The covers remained tied to their masts, the pre-eminent Wimbledon ground-staff spent all day on stand-by, the skies rallied once, then clouded over again, rains fell, and only the indomitable spirit of the British tennis public prevented wholesale hysteria. The weather was the story once more, but there was no diminution in the space allotted in the newspapers and, as ever, such situations called for an investigative snout.

It was good to see that the Spaniards had taken grass seriously for once. There were 17 men in the main draw and nine more tried to qualify, of which one had been successful. A quartet including Juan Carlos Ferrero and Albert Costa, two former French Open champions, had spent the period between Paris and SW19 scuffing their feet and honing their strokes on a grass court in Barcelona.

Carlos Moya said that if he had taken Wimbledon as seriously over the years as Tim Henman had done on the clay, he might have had the kind of result – a place in the semi-finals at Roland Garros – Henman had just enjoyed. "I didn't give myself enough time to get used to the surface but that is going to change," he said.

Up in the players lounge, there was much prowling, card games, book reading, puzzles and puzzled looks. Andy Roddick, the No.2 seed, caught my eye and bounded over for a chat, as is his wont. "I don't know if I can stand much of this," he said. "Man, I've just got to be doing something. We aren't supposed to live like this."

Roddick had appeared on the hit BBC TV show *The Weakest Link* the Friday before The Championships and, given he uncompromising nature of the show, not to mention its caustic host, it was intriguing to wonder how many other players of his stature about to play in a major championship would open themselves up to the prospect of such ridicule: Jimmy Connors, Bjorn Borg, Ivan Lendl? Do me a favour. Roddick said he didn't mind in the least, which went to the heart of his nature and competitive instinct. Not knowing that a female sheep was called a "ewe" and instead going "baaa" when he couldn't think of the answer, had endeared him to a whole new raft of the British public.

It set my mind thinking about a conversation we had shared on the Saturday before the championships about American Express's willingness to donate £25 to Sport Relief for every ace served on Centre and No.1 Court during the fortnight. As Roddick had set a record of 153mph for a serve at Queen's Club two weeks earlier, he would probably top the poll. "It's a great cause and I'm up for it," Roddick said. But, equally, he knew that everything was possible in this sport, a bad day and it will be goodbye. "Let's put it this way," he says, "the worst thing that could happen to me is to lose in the first round of Wimbledon, fly home on Wednesday, be back in my nice house surrounded by a family that loves me. That's not a bad worse case scenario, I definitely realise that."

It is because Roddick is such a natural, normal guy in an unnatural world that the difficulty some have in embracing him should be a cause for him to wonder what he has done wrong. "I'm very brash, there's no doubt," he says. "I've done some stuff on the court that can be taken two ways, it's either great for the game or this kid's a brat. Take it for what it's worth.

"But I love having fun out there; if I am two sets down and see something that makes me laugh, I'll have a joke about it. I'm not out there to please people but I don't do things for the wrong reason. I try to be as natural as possible. Charles Barkley [the basketball phenomenon] has written a book and one chapter is titled 'The 50/50 Rule'. If there's 6,000 people waiting for you after a match and you spend 90 minutes signing for 3,000 autographs and you've got to go home then, there's 3,000 who are going to be upset at you. That makes sense to me."

It helps, too, that his mother Blanche, father Jerry and a couple of older brothers take him for what he is – a young man for whom superstar status means little. "My parents aren't involved on the tour, they make sure my future is OK, but they don't feel the need to join the circus, to shake hands, kiss babies, all that stuff. They just want to know that I'm fine." Today he was fine, but fidgety.

Above: Andy Roddick is far from the weakest link on the grass of SW19.

Quote of the day

"Venus is one of the greatest tennis players and no one can beat Venus if Venus wants to play, no matter who they are. When Venus wants to play, Venus is untouchable. And what about Wayne Rooney – the 18 year old kid for England? That kid is phenomenal. He is going to sell out everything. I'm his fan already."
Richard Williams

THE CHAMPIONSHIPS
WIMBLEDON

THURSDAY 24 JUNE

Day 4

Above: Karolina Sprem can scarcely believe her victory over Venus Williams in the second round.
Opposite: Venus focuses on the ball – and not the scoreboard – during her controversial defeat.

Quote of the day

"It's not a whole barrel of laughs. Sometimes I do lose track of the score, and I just felt that maybe, maybe I had lost track again. I don't question a lot of calls. I just played and did my best on that point. I'd like to think one point doesn't make a difference."
Venus Williams

AFTER the bitter frustrations of Wednesday, the sun peeped back over the spire of St Mary's on the morning of the 24th. Bits of blue were spotted amid fluffy white clouds, and the prospect of a full day's play was as inviting as the landscape of these delightful grounds. Andy Roddick, thankfully for his own sanity and those of the people in his twitchy coterie, got to play. Then Venus Williams lost in the most bizarre circumstances imaginable.

Roddick defeated Yeu-Tzuoo (known as Jimmy) Wang from Chinese Taipei, 6-3, 7-5, 6-4, but had been given a tougher time than he might have wanted from a player about whom we should hear much more. Roddick, though, dominated when he had to and won in straight sets. Williams went out to Karolina Sprem of Croatia on Centre Court in a match that was to have considerable repercussions.

It had been a splendid match even before the second set tie-break, the outcome of which was odd in the extreme. With the score at 1-2, the first serve of Sprem was called wide. Venus, though, struck the ball back as if by instinct and Sprem, following through, played the ball into the open court. Umpire Ted Watts called 2-2, when it should have been a second serve. No one moved, the players looked up but said nothing, not a linesperson stirred. In the BBC commentary box, John Barrett's normally warm, cosy voice, rose to a crescendo: "This is one of the most extraordinary things I've ever seen in tennis."

Watts, subsequently, did not notice the players were standing the wrong side of the lines, the scoring went on and Sprem was called a winner having been given a point that wasn't hers to accept. Williams went on her way, making as little fuss as possible, which was to her immense credit.

A grand slam champion beaten in straight sets by a British player ranked No.479 should provoke an onrush of the vapours. But Mark Hilton appeared highly embarrassed to be asked to stand in the middle of Court No.3 and raise his fists in a victory salute. Such triumphalism does not come easily to those who spend their lives travelling economy class, and living in whatever B&B they can find. Hilton was stopped a couple of times on his

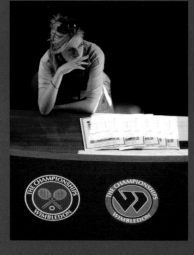

Top: Italian Davide Sanguinetti reaches for a backhand against homeboy Greg Rusedski.
Above: Rusedski retruns the compliment with a deep slice.
Above left: Mark Hilton powers a forehand during his shock win over Spain's Albert Costa.
Left: Costa's struggles on grass continued against the young Briton.
Far left: The official tournament programme on the verge of selling out.
Over: Goran Ivanisevic

Game of the day
Karol Beck v Jonny Marray 6-4, 6-7, 4-6, 6-3, 10-8

way back to the locker room and asked to sign his name and duly accommodated the well-wishers with a flash of pen across paper. It would be nice to think his scrawls might be worth something in a few years time. For that to happen, the 23-year-old from Mickle Trafford in Cheshire has to regard his 6-1, 6-4, 6-3 win over Albert Costa – a Spaniard whose aversion to grass meant he had not even bothered to board a plane to London for the past four years – as an indication of what he could do more often if he got his head down and gave the sport his all.

From first to last against the 2002 French Open champion, Hilton was in the ascendant, the little guy taking it to the big name with gusto, application and a variety of angles. He crafted winners and offered pugnacious defence, which made one wonder why he was thinking of quitting tennis altogether a few months ago. Hilton had led 5-1 when the light died on Tuesday, a set of such appalling ineptitude by Costa that Jose Perlas, his long-time coach, screamed at him that he hadn't come over from Spain to see his player not even trying.

Costa said that he would definitely try when they re-started and when he led 3-1 in the second set, he looked to be making good on

that word. But Hilton refused to be cowed, rather gritting his teeth and setting Costa so many puzzles that the Spaniard actually came in to volley behind his first serve on two occasions, something he had probably never done before. Hilton must have known then that he had a real chance.

Hilton finally secured victory with a superb backhand return of serve that, in turn, set up a stinging backhand pass that Costa stunned into the net. "He knows how to play on grass, he knew perfectly what to do at every moment," was Costa's gracious assessment.

And still it was not over for Goran Ivanisevic. If his victory over Youzhny on the opening day was not intriguing enough, the fact that the committee decided to put him on Court No.2 for his second round against Filippo Volandri of Italy, stirred the prospects of unhappy endings. When he went two sets to one down and the blond Italian was striking the ball with such vigour, Ivanisevic knew he had to draw upon some special resolve to prevail. Something got him going; probably the surroundings, the atmosphere, the crowd. "I didn't want to lose, this is a match that you don't want to lose," he said. "Sure I was happy at the end, I wanted to throw the chair, even with the umpire in it! I came through."

In the weeks preceding the championships, at both Queen's Club and Nottingham, Jonny Marray (above) had demonstrated that his rush-the-net game could reap enormous dividends on grass. It was the kind of tactic best sharpened if matches went quickly, but this one, against Karol Beck, the man who had beaten Tim Henman in the Stella Artois, was a real cliff-hanger. And how close Marray, from Sheffield, came to downing the talented Slovak – three match points in the fifth set, the last of which, a forehand he would make nine times out of ten, came back to hurt him.

But Marray had certainly earned his wild card with a surge up the men's rankings that saw him climb over 300 places to be No.230 by the time the championships had reached a conclusion. It fit well with the LTA's desire for individual improvement and the rewards that could be earned if someone put their heart and soul into the sport.

Clockwise from top left: Tommy Haas, Stefan Koubek, Vincent Spadea, Sjeng Schalken, Woodbridge & Bjorkman in the mens' doubles, Rainer Schuettler and Andy Roddick.

Shock of the day
Guillermo Coria wins at SW19

The boys' doubles champion in 1999 (with David Nalbandian) completed and, for the first time, won a singles match at Wimbledon. Indeed, the Argentine (above) knew that if he won the first two points of the day on No.1 Court the match would be his – and he didn't disappoint. His debut victory in three attempts took four days to complete. Its final flourish was 45 seconds. Coria defeated Wesley Moodie, a South African qualifier, 6-4, 6-7, 6-3, 6-7, 6-3 in a match that not only involved the sun rising three times but during which Coria estimated he had watched at least five full length feature films.

It is not as if Coria's recent history has been without incident. He lost in the final of the French Open to Gaston Gaudio, having been two sets up, and then went out in the opening round of the Stella Artois two days later to Yen-Hsun Lu of Taipei. Next, he flew to Holland and reached the final of Rosmalen before heading to Wimbledon for a match on the opening day. It was incredible that he knew where he was, let alone could hold it together through such a marathon. The transition to grass from clay is regarded as one of the more stressful and Coria had the additional burden of the heartbreak of Roland Garros. For him to reach the semi-finals here would surely be akin to Tim Henman's recent achievements on the red brick. "It would be difficult, but I do have the self-confidence," he said. "The public here have treated me really well. It makes you happy when you feel you are supported by the people."

FRIDAY 25 JUNE

Day 5

Main: Goran Ivanisevic, replete with Croatian football shirt, applauds the crowd after his defeat by Lleyton Hewitt. Below, top to bottom: Happpy campers. The obligatory queues at the All England Club gates.

THE CHAMPIONSHIPS
WIMBLEDON

Day 5 • Sharapova v Hantuchova

The Wimbledon world began to take note of Maria Sharapova. For the first time in her career, the 17 year-old from Russia was invited on to Centre Court. There she was to meet Slovakian Daniela Hantuchova, an opponent who knew exactly what it was like to clamber upon the tennis wheel of fortune – and to occasionally lose her balance in the process.

Hantuchova had undergone all sorts of minute examinations of her form, and the fluctuation in her body weight had caused some to worry that she had become far too thin. Throughout it all, Hantuchova – a treasure of a girl – dismissed the fears, and had returned earlier in the year to work with Nigel Sears, her British coach, and things seemed on the mend. She was looking and playing well and, having reached the final at Eastbourne the week before the championships, there was justification in her belief that she would have a good fortnight.

But Sharapova had retained her Birmingham title and, having received a wild card last year, was in the event by right with a seeding of No.13. The two of them lit up the stage as they entered, but the match itself would not live up to its billing as Sharapova swept her opponent aside with a breathtaking performance, mounted on supreme self-confidence. "Point after point, I really had to fight for it," Sharapova said, emphasising the manner in which she played her tennis, with a ferocity remarkable in one so young. She reminded one of Boris Becker who performed with so few inhibitions at the same age.

Sharapova was asked what might make her smile on the court. "I don't want to let my focus go," she said. "But I was enjoying every moment of it, believe me."

Elsewhere, the Russians were not quite so radiant. Anastasia Myskina had to meet Amy Frazier, the 31 year-old from Michigan who had missed only one Wimbledon since 1988 and was appearing in her 62nd grand slam. Three appearances in the fourth round was her best achievement on grass, and in 1995 she had reached a career high ranking of No.13. In 2001, Frazier had beaten the three-time French Open champion Arantxa Sanchez Vicario in the second round of Roland Garros, but had never toppled a reigning grand slam title-holder.

This was the moment for a female Frazier to punch her weight. Myskina did all she could but could not deny the American her 4-6, 6-4, 6-4 victory. "Every year I walk in here and it's the same," she said, "you can really believe you're at Wimbledon. It's exactly how you picture it. It is so special."

Day 5 · Ivanisevic v Hewitt

Match of the day

Goran Ivanisevic v Lleyton Hewitt

And so, at last, it was time to say goodbye to a Wimbledon legend. Goran Ivanisevic had played in four finals, lost the first three and at the Champions' Parade in 2000, when he was rewarded for those finals, he looked the unhappiest man alive. A year later, he was to touch the stars. The 2001 champion said that 2004 would be his last year and when he lost to the man who succeeded him, he rightly said there was no shame and that the story could not have ended much better. Hewitt was a touch too strong in all departments: he moved better, returned well and had a fire in his heart that Ivanisevic could not match. "I didn't do anything wrong, he played great," Ivanisevic said after his 6-2, 6-3, 6-4 defeat. Then, Ivanisevic looked around, looked up, and remembered what the place had meant to him. In the player's box, his father Srdjan shook hands with Glynn Hewitt, a smile wreathing his face. They knew what it meant to have champions for sons.

"Best place, best court, it couldn't have been better," Goran said. "And [Hewitt] said it was an honour to play me and when someone like him says that, I'm very proud of myself. I lost to a guy who can win any time if he plays like this."

Right: Goran Ivanisevic reflects on his last ever appearance on Centre Court.
Below: Goran gives it his all as the curtain comes down on a remarkable career.
Bottom left: Lleyton Hewitt pays tribute to the charismatic Croat.

Day 5 Rusedski v Schuettler

This page, clockwise: Xavier Malisse, Carlos Moya, Juan-Carlos Ferrero, Jennifer Capriati, Todd Martin and Tommy Haas.

Opposite page, top to bottom: Greg Rusedski, Paola Suarez and Serena Williams.

It wasn't so special for Greg Rusedski this time around. The British No.2 had simply not played enough – a drugs charge, of which he was later cleared, had eaten into his heart and spirit. Indeed, the episode may well yet contribute to a hastening of the end of his career – and he was never able to last the distance against someone as eager and fastidious as Rainer Schuettler. At the conclusion of the German's 6-7, 7-6, 6-7, 6-2, 6-2 victory, there seemed an awful lot more between the two than a couple of years.

The wild card Rusedski received into Wimbledon had more to do with the championships looking after one of their own than anything he had done in the previous year to merit the reward. He knew he was going through a difficult time and would have beaten Schuettler had this been a best of three set match. He came out of two of the three tie-breaks with the knowledge that his serve – especially his old faithful, the swinger wide into the advantage court – remained one of the most potent in tennis. But this is the sport at the long haul and Rusedski found it all extremely demanding. Schuettler eventually wore him down; indeed Rusedski's body had to be twisted and bent into all sorts of uncomfortable looking positions by an ATP trainer to get him back out and fit to play. One correspondent described it as "osteopathic manipulation." It did not quite do the trick.

Quote of the day

"I have discussed the incident with the umpire and we agreed it was in the best interests of both parties if he takes no further part in the event." **Wimbledon referee Alan Mills** on Ted Watts, the umpire who incorrectly awarded Karolina Sprem a point during a tie-break in her match against Venus Williams. Watts offered to stand down from The Championships, a gesture that had been accepted.

Number One Court enjoying some much-needed sun.

COURT No.13

PREVIOUS SETS	PLAYER	SETS	GAMES	POINTS
	M. KNOWLES			
	D. NESTOR			
	R. GINEPRI			
	M. MERKLEIN			

THE CHAMPIONSHIPS
WIMBLEDON

SATURDAY 26 JUNE

Day 6

Day 6

Above: Sir Roger Bannister passes the Olympic Torch to Tim Henman.

ANOTHER complete washout, the second in four days and the scene inside the grounds was of woe unconfined. Tennis writers were left to hang around the club all day with nothing to do but re-hash old tales and watch re-runs of the re-runs they had watched all day Wednesday. The loudest cheer went up in the press room at 5.45pm when the covers were drawn back across the court for the final time; all the pages had been filled with features and interviews and no one wanted the chore of having to cover live play so late in the day.

My colleague on *The Times,* Giles Smith, was watching at home and duly reported that the news of a "People's Sunday" was broken by Garry Richardson, the BBC's ace investigative reporter, during *Grandstand*. In a fearless interview conducted under a dripping umbrella on Centre Court, Richardson cornered Chris Gorringe, the Chief Executive of the All England Club, and, without pausing to soften him up with a few easy ones, put the question that was on an entire nation's lips: "Will there be play tomorrow?"

Yes, he confirmed, there would. Ten thousand tickets for the Centre Court would be available on a first-come, first-served basis at £35 each. Eleven thousand tickets for No.1 Court would be available similarly, priced at £30. In addition, 7,000 ground passes would be on sale. These were to be priced at £15 each. The queuing would be in a northerly direction from Southfields, Gorringe continued. Please only come if you live relatively locally, he requested, and be sure to travel light to facilitate the bag-searching process.

Notice formally served, we found ourselves on the verge of a significant, or at any rate infrequent, event: tennis on a middle Sunday for only the third time in the history of The Championships. You could sense Richardson's spirits quickening. A "People's Sunday" means people, and people mean vox pop interviews. And vox pop interviews mean Richardson putting a microphone under the nose of someone in the front row and asking, "Where have you come from?", which he clearly loves to do.

Gorringe, on the other hand, made no effort to disguise the fact that he had reservations. Not, you understand, on account of any mixed feelings the All England Club might have about admitting "the people", either literally or, indeed, as a concept, and not at the prospect of great clumps of the unwashed moving among the club's rather lovely flower beds; but because of the logistics. "As I'm standing here," he said, "I'm not too excited about it."

You wouldn't catch Sue Barker, the BBC anchor, saying that kind of thing. True, Sue doesn't have to liaise with the police and catering services in order to get an extra day's play off the ground at 24 hours' notice. But even if she did, and if she were additionally held personally responsible for security on the day, I hazard her enthusiasm for a "People's Sunday" would be undimmed. Sue, you get the impression, would gladly have a "People's Sunday" even if it was Monday.

"A party atmosphere guaranteed!" she told the viewers. Opposite her, John Lloyd was similarly grinning with pleasure. "They're the real fans, when they come and queue up for hours," he said. Well, up to a point. But if we're going to persist in calling it "People's Sunday", what are we going to call all those days from last week? Non-Person's Thursday? The Disqualified's Friday? And if, as Lloyd says, these are the "real fans", then what does that make the people who queued up or bought tickets for all the other days?

Where were Sunday's off-the-cuff show-ups when last week's visitors were filling out their ballot forms, posting their money a year in advance and organising their summer holidays around the dates of the championships? Where were the drop-ins

when people were investing their hard-earned savings in debentures? Without doubt, the Sunday crowd would contain its share of dispossessed diehards, grabbing with both hands the rare opportunity to feed their obsession. But there was equally no getting away from the fact that their number would include, by definition, chancers, day-trippers and tourists brought out by the sunshine.

Left: Some typical British stoicism in the face of more rain.
Below: The order of play would remain static throughout Day 6.

THE CHAMPIONSHIPS WIMBLEDON

SUNDAY 27 JUNE

Middle Sunday

By 8.30am, the queue was 10,000 strong and as each half hour dragged by, it grew in length until it snaked through Wimbledon Park and beyond. Getting into the grounds was, at best, a protracted process but no one on the outside wanting to get in seemed to mind. There was eager anticipation everywhere. Into the teeth of People's Sunday marched Tim Henman, who showed his full set, beaming broadly as he stepped onto Centre Court.

Henman's opponent, Hicham Arazi, had known ecstatic home support the last time the pair had met, in a Davis Cup tie in Casablanca. Then, the Moroccan prevailed in the opening singles and set the tone for a North African success. This time, there were only a couple of folk wearing fezes and even they spoke with English accents.

The day before, as part of the celebrations marking the arrival of the Olympic flame in London for the first time in decades, Henman had been happy to accept the torch from Sir Roger Bannister, the first man to break the four-minute mile barrier 50 years earlier.

To the chagrin of many observers, Henman's torch-bearing leg of the relay actually included running up and down two flights of very slippery steps – and he started against Arazi as if he hasn't wiped the damp from the soles of his shoes. A service break to love in the third game, as Arazi's racket gave off that distinctive fizzing sound while sighing echoed through the rows of seats still to be occupied at the top of the court.

The Great Britain No.1 managed to break serve in the eighth game, but sacrificed a lead in the tie-break with two horrid backhand volleys. Henman's touch returned on a third and Arazi netted, but the little Moroccan still created a set point, only for Henman's volley to work this time. The best shot of the entire match was the forehand lob Henman contrived on his first set point – glorious finesse and fortitude under pressure. So how could it go from that to Henman losing another service game to love to trail 4-2 in the second? And what happened to Arazi when he lost 13 points in a row for Henman to break back twice, competently serving out for a two set lead?

ORDER OF PLAY

SUNDAY 27th JUNE

2004

Top: A sight to delight many – play on the
middle Sunday for only the third time in history.
Above: Hicham Arazi tries to spoil the party.
Left: After a slow, slightly nervous start,
Tim Henman finally gets his volley to work.

Centre Court: Henman serves under blue skies and in a carnival atmosphere.

Match of the day

Florian Mayer bt Wayne Ferreira 4-6, 6-4, 6-1, 6-4.

The significance of the match was more important than the levels of quality it reached. It was likely that this was the last of Wayne Ferreira's 43 singles matches at Wimbledon in his 55th consecutive grand slam, a record of endurance that may never be beaten. For Mayer, a 20-year-old leading member of the advancing guard of German tennis, it was a notable scalp; if we had learned anything from the South African down the year, it is that he never relinquished his position in a tournament without taking his opponent down to the wire.

"I'd like to come back and watch at least," Ferreira said, "And I'd like to bring my son [five year-old Marcus] when he's a little bit bigger, when he understands what it's all about." Best he had ever faced? "Agassi." Best venue? "Here." "I've just been privileged to spend 15 years on the circuit doing something that I've loved."

Opposite: Roger Federer in imperious form against former Australian Open champion Thomas Johansson.
Inset: Johansson was forced to play most of the game at full stretch.

The last few rallies offered Henman at his best – a running forehand pass to snatch Arazi's serve at 3-2 brought his coach Paul Annacone to his feet in a rare display of fist-pumping fervour – and his most clumsy, when a smash off the rim landed first bounce into the stands. Still, he made it, reflexes steady, heart rate less so.

Roger Federer had got the crowd into the mood by booking his place in the last 16 with a straight set victory over Thomas Johansson, the 2002 Australian Open champion. The defending champion was beginning to look in ominous form, and though Johansson was straining to become the challenger of old – he had missed seven months of the previous year following shoulder surgery and was finding the edge hard to rediscover – he was not someone who gifted a single point. Federer's place in the last eight, a 6-3, 6-4, 6-3 victory, was not earned without breaking sweat. His demeanour throughout, though, was of a man sure he would win.

Federer's service had still not been broken and he remarked that when he was break point down a couple of times, he made his first serve hit the button. With that part of his game in a grove, he could take more risks on his second serve. "And that is when I really start to play well," he said. Uh-oh.

Mark Philippoussis, too, was moving into the radar at a rate of knots. The 2003 losing finalist had not won a single match on tour between the third round of the Australian Open and the opening round of Wimbledon. Only the previous week he had lost to Ian Flanagan, a British player ranked No.840 in the world. The mighty Philippoussis looked seriously out-of-sorts.

But a 6-4, 6-1, 6-7, 7-5 victory over the hard-hitting Chilean Fernando Gonzalez was a real tonic. Not only that, it set him up the following day for a fourth round meting with Tim Henman. Philippoussis didn't lose his serve once against Gonzalez, served 27 aces, and was striking the ball with enormous power. "I definitely believe I will win here one day," he said. "That Centre Court, there's no other that has the same feeling, or looks as good."

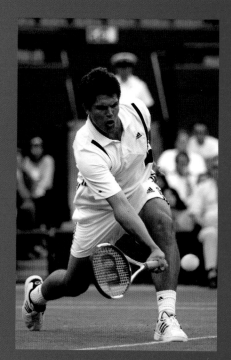

Above: Philippoussis Snr and Delta Goodrem look on anxiously.
Right: Amelie Mauresmo punches through another unreturnable backhand.
Below right, clockwise from top left: Ladies' Singles winners Rita Grande, Silvia Farina Elia, Anne Kremer and Virginia Ruano Pascual.

Above: Taylor Dent bends low but bows out to compatriot Andy Roddick.
Above right: Mark Philippoussis reaches the second week again.
Right: John McEnroe still dominates Centre Court.

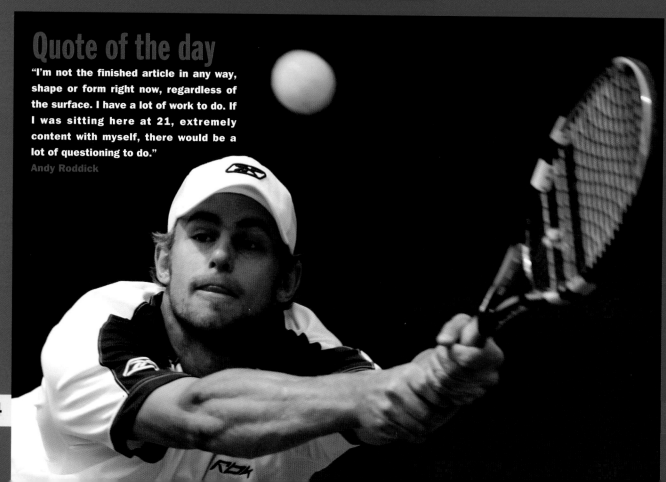

Quote of the day

"I'm not the finished article in any way, shape or form right now, regardless of the surface. I have a lot of work to do. If I was sitting here at 21, extremely content with myself, there would be a lot of questioning to do."
Andy Roddick

THE CHAMPIONSHIPS WIMBLEDON

MONDAY 28 JUNE

Day 7

Hewitt v Moya • Day 7

NO time to draw breath. For those forced to play on Sunday, the immediate task was to find a new pair of whites and get straight back out there again. The concertina effect of two days wiped from the schedule, and the desire for the two rounds of 16 to be completed by Monday, meant that to win this championship you really would have to earn your spurs.

Good matches were everywhere, standing in the alleyways was three to four deep. No court was left idle and wherever you looked something of real significance was happening; throughout the grounds was a feeling of frenzy and fun. It was one of those rare days when there was every reason to savour a ground pass as much as the embossed tickets to Centre or No.1 courts.

The two matches on Centre were truly of the highest order: Carlos Moya, indicating a readiness to go all the way on grass, was to meet Lleyton Hewitt, the 2002 champion, in a contest that would rip the top of what was left of the greenery in the back stretches of the court. Then Tim Henman would meet last year's runner-up, Mark Philippoussis. The BBC was beside itself, wondering how many viewers it would pocket at peak time for the meeting of British hero and Australian powerhouse.

The entrée was sensational. Moya and Hewitt squared off in a tremendous duel. The match-up was crystallised in the demeanour of Moya – some sort of tennis God, straight from central casting, with long bronzed limbs and a sweatband keeping back his rock-style hair – and Hewitt, who by contrast, was the squat, feisty Australian in a reverse baseball cap who bolts around the place in a distinctly caffeinated manner. The pair set about each other with the vigour demanded of their talent. This might have been the match to decide last year's Davis Cup final in Melbourne, but Philippoussis put an end to that with the Cup-winning performance over Juan Carlos Ferrero in the fourth rubber. Moya had points to make but for the first couple of sets, Hewitt was in the ascendant – even when he was on the floor he won points, as when Moya, facing a break point at 2-3 in the second set, sent a backhand lob over Hewitt and the baseline.

Moya, though, broke twice in the third, the second of which to love at 4-4 ended on the best rally of the match, slice after sliced backhand from the Spaniard until, having opened up the court to his liking, he unleashed a double-handed winner down the line. He rounded off the set with a forehand drive volley winner – the crowd delighted in that. But Hewitt, as we know, is made of stern stuff. He broke first in the fourth set, only for Moya to respond in the next game; the Spaniard saved a match point at 4-5 when Hewitt netted a backhand, leading to the inevitable thud of racket on turf. The tie-break, though, was utterly one-sided in the Australian's favour.

Then came Tim Henman, knowing that the last man to deny him a place in the quarter-finals was Mark Philippoussis in 2000. Their eagerly-awaited return did not start to draw blood until 5.40pm (another one of those late starts with which Henman and SW19 are feverishly acquainted), finishing three hours and seven minutes later when a Philippoussis backhand return gently swirled into the tramlines on Henman's backhand side. With it, Henman had won 6-2, 7-5, 6-7, 7-6 to set up a meeting with the unseeded Mario Ancic of Croatia. They had never previously played each other, but Ancic was the last man to defeat Roger Federer at Wimbledon – and indeed the last man to beat the hero of Switzerland on grass anywhere, in the opening round two years ago.

For 24 minutes, this was another Henman altogether from the one who had stood within a couple of points of going two sets down in the opening match against a Spanish grass court novice. A forehand lob, a forehand crosscourt winner for two break points on the opening Philippoussis serve and a backhand down the line on the first were struck with a cleanliness and precision he had groped for in the opening three rounds. Having being brushed aside in the opening set, Philippoussis offered greater resilience in the second and then took advantage of Henman's inevitable slack period to take the third. He had to be put away in a thoroughly professional manner in the fourth, but even then the British No.1 faltered on the threshold, losing his serve for the first time in the match at 5-3. How wildly ironic, how wildly Henman it all was.

The women's event was picking up a gear as well. An all-Asian match-up between Tamarine Tanasugarn of Thailand and Japan's Ai Sugiyama was won by the lady from Japan, whose official quote sheets were constantly interrupted by the word "smiling" in brackets. She was charm personified and a 6-3, 7-5 success suggested charm was not all she possessed. Karolina Sprem, the Croatian who had benefited from some maladroit scoring in the first week, was still alive as well, defeating Magdalena Maleeva of Bulgaria in straight sets but still having to

deal with questions from those who would not let the matter or manner of her victory over Venus Williams rest. Finally, she shot them a "I don't want to talk about this anymore," look right out of the Goran

Above: Mark Philippoussis approaches the net in a classic serve-volley encounter with Tim Henman.
Left: Defying coaches everywhere, Henman volleys without even looking at the ball.

Above: Karolina Sprem surges into the quarter-finals.
Below: Magdalena Maleeva's intense effort can't prevent defeat against Sprem.
Left: Lindsay Davenport uses her height to the maximum.

Quote of the day

"No, I don't have a boyfriend. I'm waiting for Prince William. I'll be waiting for him, sitting in the stands. There are many younger players like myself and Maria [Sharapova] who are breaking through, so get some younger people to come and watch…"

Tatiana Golovin

Left: Tatiana Golovin waits for her Prince Charming.
Below left: Thailiand's Tamarine Tanasugarn in action against Ai Sugiyama (below centre).
Bottom: Vera Zvonareva offered stiff resistance to Lindsay Davenport.

Match of the day
Donald Young bt Robin Haase 3-6, 6-2, 6-1,

What would it be that attracted Paul Annacone and Brad Gilbert (the coaches of Tim Henman and Andy Roddick respectively), Gary Swain, (John McEnroe's agent at IMG), David Felgate (the LTA's director of performance), scribes from the *New York Times* and *USA Today* and a host of clothing manufacturers to Court No.16? It was hardly as if there weren't important dates elsewhere.

A look at Donald Young, that's why. The 14 year-old from Chicago has been touted as the next big thing and here he was, all spindly legs, cap cocked to one side, left handed whipping action, playing his first round in the boy's singles. Young did not seem to remotest bit fazed by the surroundings; he overcame the loss of the opening set with a nerveless assurance and used a happy knack of being able to size up where his opponent was going to put the ball. When his game is fully developed, he is sure to be a contender.

TUESDAY 29 JUNE

Day 8

T was time to sort the wheat from the chaff. Bar the princely presence Tatiana Golovin had wanted to see, there were plenty of fresh images on Centre Court for women's quarter-final day, the moment when this section of the event started to get a bit serious. There was one face, though, that gave Golovin a bit of a fright, the one on the opposite side of the net with determination writ through it.

Serena Williams did not intend to let a 16 year-old undermine her quest for a place in the last four, and after she had won 6-2, 6-1, she professed to not having played well. "But I guess I can't complain too much, huh?" she said. One wondered how that was supposed to make young Tatiana feel.

Golovin would undoubtedly be back, stronger and more resilient to fight another time, but she had done her bit to encourage the belief that there was a groundswell of talent emerging to stiffen the challenges at the top of the game. Here was a contender of real potential to offer the French an alternative to Amelie Mauresmo's annual grand slam disappointments and the drawn-out tennis twilight of Mary Pierce.

Above: Tatiana Golovin says goodbye to the crowd after her quarter-final defeat. Left: Serena Williams contemplates another victim.

Mauresmo was still in The Championships herself, a 7-5, 6-3 victory over Silvia Farina Elia of Italy guaranteeing a second successive quarter-final on the grass. (The top half of the women's draw had fallen a round behind because of an enforced break for rain near the climax to People's Sunday). "I have a pretty good feeling and a good sensation on the surface," Mauresmo said. What is absolutely certain is that her style was a wonderful complement to, and diversion from, the many double-fisters and screamers infiltrating the higher rankings. If artistic impression were to be the difference, the No.4 seed's sweeping groundstrokes, slices and spins would win handsomely over the rest.

But, as Mauresmo knew, this is a game played more inside the head – what shot to choose, when and the mental strength to go with it – than elsewhere. "I like to think that I

**Above: Silvia Farina Elia couldn't match Amelie Mauresmo's range of shots.
Opposite: Mauresmo prepares to deliver another graceful backhand.**

Capriati v Petrova • Day 8

Match of the day
Maria Sharapova bt Ai Sugiyama 5-7, 7-5, 6-1.

Not for the first, nor the last, time at Wimbledon, were we privy to a fighting performance from the Russian who, having been at the sharp end of Sugiyama's all dashing, all thrashing tennis, managed to hold her game together and peak at just the right time. Sugiyama, the No.8 seed, was too tough early on but once Sharapova showed she was not going to be out-hit and started to make the Japanese player reach even further into the corners, another upset was on the cards. "Her serves and returns were too deep and too good in the end," Sugiyama said. But it had been a terrific tournament for the perennially happy girl from Japan, who had won the doubles the previous year with Kim Clijsters.

Maria Sharapova celebrates another scalp. Bottom: Nadia Petrova succumbs to Jennfier Capriati in the last eight.

play pure tennis," she says. "And I think the English public have a good feel for that. It is a relief sometimes to get out of Paris – not to be 'the one.' For me, I think the step is to win one of the three grand slams outside Paris – that might make the process there easier. I would love it to happen here at Wimbledon, with the game I have, especially on the grass, I have to go for it."

Much was the same attitude that had prevailed through Jennifer Capriati's career. There had never been any holding back where Capriati was concerned and it was hard to imagine we were 14 years on from the first time she had appeared at Wimbledon; then, she was aged 14 and reached the fourth round – losing to a certain Steffi Graf.

Capriati had brought another Russian's challenge to a close, defeating Nadia Petrova 6-4, 6-4; nothing surprising there, but a look up into the player's box and there was no sign of her father Stefano, who had been such a defining force in her career. Nor Heinz Guenthardt, who once coached Graf, and who had not been kept on in the Capriati camp for too long. Mr Capriati had preferred to stay home and had asked former US Davis Cup captain Tom Gullikson to see what he could do to help Capriati out. The acid test would come now, against Williams in the semi-finals.

"It's never really been about the person, it's my tennis against the other person's tennis. That stuff about the aura, the mystique, the personality, never really plays a part." Jennifer Capriati, on the prospect of playing the redoubtable Serena Williams in the semi-final.

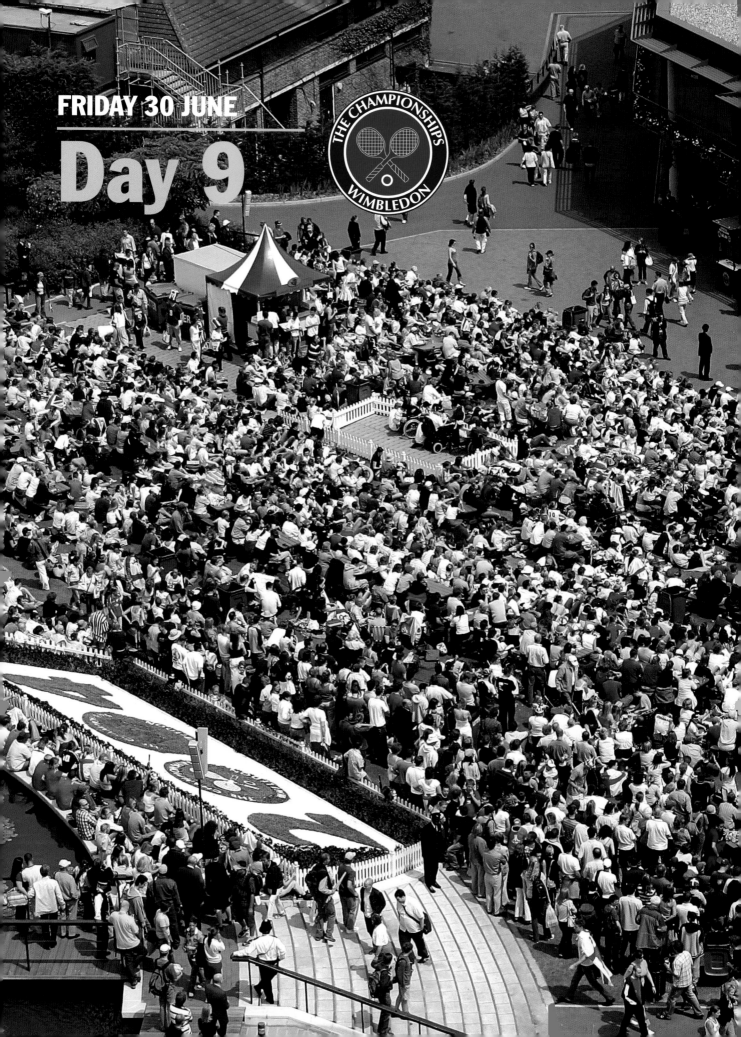

FRIDAY 30 JUNE

Day 9

THE CHAMPIONSHIPS
WIMBLEDON

Day 9 • Henman v Ancic

Quote of the day

"I've never hidden behind the fact that this is the tournament I'd like to win the most, and the reality is that I don't have an endless number of years or chances left. Losing gets worse, actually, as years go by. I'm sure my desire, dedication and motivation will always be there. You need time to step back, switch off and let time be a healer. But there is no consolation."

Tim Henman

The previous evening, the engaging 20 year-old Mario Ancic had been seated with me at one of the tables on the second floor balcony of the Media Centre, pondering his quarter-final against Tim Henman. "I think tomorrow is going to be as good as it gets," Ancic said, with a distinctive air that suggested eager-beaverishness and a cold-eyed determination in equal measure. As good as it gets, he said. But for whom?

Within 24 hours we knew, and the impact had its usual polarising effect on the home nation. Ancic was standing in the middle of the Centre Court where, two years earlier, he had been the last man to beat Roger Federer on grass. First, the Croatian puffed out his cheeks, then he stood stock still, mouth agape, exalting his coach, Rohan Goetzkee (who had inspired Dutchman Richard Krajicek to the title in 1996); he was in his own wonderland.

On the opposite side of the net, Henman was walking slowly towards him, right hand outstretched, jaw clenched, ambition crushed. Ancic had defeated the Briton 7-6, 6-4, 6-4, a defeat for which there was only one consolation, that it was no slow, drawn out closure, for which Henman was probably grateful.

In *The Times*, Simon Barnes reflected on "a gloriously gloomy occasion. It is not Henman's fault that the British hope too much, the fault lies with the hopers, not the hopee. He faced the bleakness of defeat and did not blink. He knows that, if we are all saved, we will all be back again next year, hoping that this year is the year."

The first break point against Ancic was saved with a 131mph ace and Henman did not have the sniff of another until Ancic suddenly showed a touch of nerves, double faulting twice to relinquish the break he had earned in the fifth game of the second set. It was then that the Briton had to impose himself, but he promptly lost his next serve to love, missing a sit-up-and-beg forehand volley, before being nailed by a couple of superb returns and plunging a low volley into the net from another rapier-like return.

Though Henman's volleying was, initially, every bit as crisp as it had been against Philippoussis in the previous round, Ancic is a better mover than the Australian. He reached more of Henman's shots and managed to contrive some fabulous winners, not least off the forehand wing. The volley with which the Croatian secured the second set, from below the top of the net, racket steady, angle perfect, was evidence of his preparedness for victory.

The third set did not last long enough to be described as interesting. In the third game, Henman double faulted, a forehand service return almost spun the racket from his hand and another clinched the break. The killer blow was a flashing backhand crosscourt from one of those high backhand volleys with which Henman always seems to nail a winner of his own. Once he served to the Ancic forehand on the first break point, it was all up.

As ever, the post mortem was long and detailed. It involved things said about Henman that, with an ounce more common sense, would not have been said. The simple truth was that, on this day, he was soundly second best and took his medicine like a man. A week later, he was to receive an OBE from the Queen. All was (almost) forgotten.

Ancic would play Andy Roddick, who had crept up on the blindside of the field – he was the No.2 and Queen's champion, yet had reached this stage without making much of a fuss – but managed to hold sway against Sjeng

Day 9 • Schalken v Roddick

Right: Andy Roddick can't hide his delight at reaching another Grand Slam semi.
Below: Wimbledon nearly-man Sjeng Schalken suffered another tough loss, this time to Roddick.

Schalken, the Dutchman who had made a habit of reaching the second week. Roddick won 7-6, 7-6, 6-3, a result behind which there was a touching story to tell. On the eve of the Telecom Italia Masters in Rome in May, a fire had broken out in the Parco dei Principe hotel, which promised to engulf the floors above Roddick's room on the seventh. One of the perks of having a de-luxe suite was a balcony twice the size of most and Roddick, cognisant of the danger above, pushed his mattress out and pleaded with those above him to use it as soft landing area on which they could leap. Schalken and his wife Ricky were two of those rescued.

It was impossible for the two men not to be linked forever from that day. They had a thread that could never be broken, no matter what might occur on a tennis court. Roddick said he preferred to forget that it ever happened, but he knew he could not. Schalken, a splendid competitor, saw an opponent, but also a saviour. That he played so well, struck the ball so fiercely, but could not quite manage to win and reach his first grand slam semi-final, meant plenty to the Dutchman. That he was here at all meant an awful lot more.

Watching Roddick is, someone said, akin to gathering round a test-your-strength fairground game with a mallet and pole. Maybe the All England Club should go all the way and put a bell on the on-court speedometer, set to ding at speeds of 142mph. Fun for all the family!

Match of the day

Roger Federer v Lleyton Hewitt

A repeat of their meeting at the Australian Open in January – also won by Federer – this one was to include a couple of those sets that took your breath away. When Hewitt broke Federer in the fourth set, it was the first time in the championship that it had happened to the Swiss, yet Hewitt did not win another game. And when was the last time in a best of five set match that the Australian had lost two sets 6-0 and 6-1?

Eventually, he was simply worn down by Federer's sustained brilliance. The top seed won 6-1, 6-7, 6-0, 6-4 and qualified for a semi-final against Sebastien Grosjean of France. The one element from this match that stood out was that however well Hewitt played – and he did so fantastically – Federer was able to raise his game one further level.

Above: Hewitt receives treatment – to his thigh, and maybe his morale.

Day 9

Right: Amelie Mauresmo celebrates.
Below: Paola Suarez. Bottom: Florian Mayer
enjoys some evening sunshine.

Sebastien Grosjean secures his
place against Roger Federer in
the men's quarter-finals.

Davenport v Sharapova • Day 10

Below: Rain interrupted the see-saw semi between former champion Lindsay Davenport and rising star Maria Sharapova.
Right: Sharapova is all smiles after her three set victory.

THERE were four fascinating stories to relate from this day's play. Serena Williams, still searching for that special something she had missed during her eight-month isolation from competition; Amelie Mauresmo, freed from the shackles of France and ready to become a grand slam champion; Lindsay Davenport, openly speculating that this might be her last year on the circuit, time and

tiresome schedules having taken their toll; and Maria Sharapova, loving every coruscating moment of this great adventure.

First things first. Davenport against Sharapova was the meeting of a player who had grown weary of the travails of tennis and all that it took from the body and mind (and yes, she is only 28) and a player 11 years her junior, who faced every day with a smile – though not when she was in the middle of business on the court.

Sharapova had torn into this championship with a rare frenzy. She had worried not a jot for reputations and Davenport knew nothing was likely to change in the semi-final either. There are few pleasures in sport to compare with the arrival of a brave new talent, someone who's got it. And the younger they are, the better it all is.

We had seen Sharapova for five rounds now and said "maybe" and "we'll see" and enjoyed observing the free running, the free swinging, and in previous rounds, the clear indication that she had the stomach for a fight. But now she faced a one-time champion in Davenport, albeit one who hadn't been back to a grand slam final since the Australian Open in 2000. In the beginning, Davenport was awesome, serving too big, hitting too heavy, too deep and too consistent. She had a stronger mind, her competitive nerve in better training.

That was the first set and the first two games of the second. Davenport had a couple of points for a 3-0 lead which she couldn't take – Sharapova rallied to 2-1 and then the rains came. Now rains at Wimbledon are the stuff of legend: it is about coping, it is about concentrating, it is about using all the time behind the scenes to the best of your ability. Sharapova? Sharapova read magazines. Not only that, she read magazines she wasn't exactly fascinated by.

What would have happened had she returned 3-0 down nobody will ever know. The rains had gone, Sharapova began to shine. She went for her second serve with greater gusto and the second set headed into a tie-break. Davenport won the first point on a mini-break, Sharapova responded in kind with two of her own, double-faulted and struck a backhand long: 3-3. Then she rushed off three straight points but Davenport clawed her way back,

MISS L. DAVENPORT
V
MISS M. SHARAPOVA

only for Sharapova to strike an inside-out backhand into the corner.

Once that was done, she ran away with the final set to conclude a 2-6, 7-6, 6-1 victory, one that took Davenport's breath away. "When we came back from the rain break, she started to serve much better and, unfortunately, I began to serve a lot worse," the former champion said. "I don't feel like I gave away the match at all – I lost to someone who rose to the challenge today.

"It is bitter-sweet to walk away off a court and a venue where I've had great victories and some great moments in my career. I've had an amazing career, a very long one. No, I don't think I'll be back."

And so to a semi-final that promised even more. Mauresmo had been waiting for this moment since she was trounced 6-2, 6-1 at the same stage by Serena two years earlier. The French No.4 seed was determined that she would not be blown away to such an extent this time around. And so unfolded a brilliant match.

Mauresmo, having lost her first service game, trailed throughout the first set until she broke back with a half smash on her second break point in the tenth game. She trailed in the tie-break too, but a fierce exchange of forehands at 5-4 saw the ball whiz from side to side, but it was the French girl who promptly pocketed the set. She led 3-1 and had 0-30 on the Williams serve in the second, the champion actually broke the rim of her racket in one show of disgust. Something got her going.

Mauresmo was slipping a little and went off for five minutes of treatment to rub some life into her ailing back – a cause of problems before. Williams could not have expected her to come out with such freedom and she did not like it, but still held on to take the match into a deciding set where Mauresmo had a point for a 3-1 lead. Once more, an opportunity slid by and you wondered how many she might need.

Eventually the Mauresmo service gave out in the tenth game, a final forehand bounced wide and Williams had claimed a 6-7, 7-5, 6-4 victory in two hours, 27 minutes. "I would love to reach a final again like five years ago in Australia," Mauresmo said. "I'm getting closer and closer." And, one felt sadly, further and further away.

**Above: Amelie Mauresmo receives treament for her injured back.
Right: Serena Williams smashes her way into another final.**

Quote of the day

"I shall prepare in a way I shan't tell you The lion is the king of the forest but the tiger is the king of the jungle."
Serena Williams on her preparation to play Maria Sharapova in the final.

Top: Contrasting emotions as Amelie Mauresmo contemplates her semi-final defeat while Serena (below) jumps for joy. **Right:** Mauresmo demonstrates her all-court game.

Day 11 · Grosjean v Federer

WHEN you are stuck in the midst of the postponements and alterations, you automatically assume it can never have been this bad before. But we should remember that over the years Wimbledon has got used to flying by the seat of its perfectly-creased pants.

The Club purchased its first tarpaulin in 1890 at a cost of £60. In 1912, it rained on most days and The Championships was held over until the third Monday; seven years later, it was not completed until the third Tuesday. The reason for the event being extended in 1925 was to give the two singles finalists, Rene Lacoste and Jean Borotra, time to rest before they paired for the doubles final. 1927 was one of the wettest meetings ever, with another third Tuesday finish. In 1958 – recorded as a "very wet fortnight" – the singles semi-finals were split for the first time between Centre and No.1 Court. In 1963, it was cold, miserable and wet, the rain contriving to wash out play

completely on the second Saturday, and all four finals were delayed until another Monday. And so on and so on.

There was no doubting from the weather forecast that men's semi-finals day would be tough, though three of its four participants had been there before, so the nerves should not have been too difficult to control. Roger Federer was to face Sebastien Grosjean of France; Andy Roddick to take on Mario Ancic, both matches scheduled for Centre Court. By mid-afternoon, after the third occasion when Federer (who slashed a ball high over the stand to emphasise his frustration) and Grosjean had to dash from the scene, the second semi was re-routed to No.1 court. There, those who had expected a day of doubles were fed something even more appetising.

When the day's play concluded, Federer led his opponent by two sets to love and 4-3 in the third; Roddick was a set and 4-3 ahead over Ancic but the Croatian had a

Opposite: Sebastien Grosjean finds time to serve between the showers.

Below: Fans during the rain break.

break point on the second seed's serve. What a moment to have to leave the field of play!

Grosjean's achievement of reaching the semi-finals without conceding a set did not last long once he had to face Federer's power. The Swiss broke in the first game and was comfortably holding that lead at 3-2 when the first serious interruption came after 22 minutes play. As rain persisted through the afternoon, the match was halted for four hours and 40 minutes before resumption was possible in the evening sunshine. Two aces confirmed the first set in Federer's favour.

Having reaped no reward from playing his normal baseline game, Grosjean opted to start coming in to test Federer's skills on the passing shot, a tactic that paid initial dividends. There was also the odd mis-hit coming from Federer, but these tended to lean towards too much extravagance. It did not take long for him to find the sublime touches more reminiscent of the man's talents.

Grosjean's hopes did not survive longer than the first six games of the second set as, in a flurry of glorious shots, Federer conceded a mere four points on serve and won it in 33 minutes. In the third, Federer teased his opponent; he fell love-30 behind three times, only to move into another gear. He established a 4-3 lead before the players went off again, this time for the night.

On BBC radio, Nick Mullins said: "Federer has gone back into the locker rooms to change and get into his spaceship to take off for whatever planet it is he comes from."

Celebrities of the day
Sir David Frost and Michael Parkinson

These two gentlemen, who have spent most of their lives interviewing the great and the good, had plenty to discuss with each other during splashes of play and rain delays. It is quite possible that they were fighting between themselves for the right to invite Sir Clive Woodward, the head coach of England's World Cup rugby winning side, on to their shows. Senator George Mitchell, one of the most respected American politicians, who had helped broker Northern Ireland's Good Friday Peace agreement, was also in the Royal Box to ensure fair play was adhered to at all times.

Quote of the day

"Maria (Sharapova) reminds me of me. I remember hitting with her when she was just a 12 year-old kid. You could see the potential, the burning fire, the desire even then. I don't think she will be awestruck today against Serena. I think she will show her capability. Maria is as mean as a snake."
Martina Hingis, the 1997 Wimbledon champion at 16 years of age.

Opposite: Federer took command of his unfinished match against Grosjean (left).

Roddick blasts a serve

SATURDAY 3 JULY

Day 12

Serena Williams (below) and Maria Sharapova (right) trade blows in the Ladies Singles Final.

Williams, S v Sharapova • Day 12

SATURDAY, July 3rd was not the end of Maria Sharapova's journey. At 17, she has only just begun. What happened on Centre Court on the first of the finals days, one that was witnessed by that strongest of all women, the former Prime Minister Baroness Thatcher, was a joyous announcement. From would-be, to really is. Sharapova arrived in sensational fashion. "Superpova" they called her, and with good reason.

As journeys go, stage one is complete; it was an adventure that began when she left Russia with her father Yuri, and whose first port of call was Nick Bollettieri's tennis academy in Bradenton, Florida, where they arrived uninvited and extremely under-funded. She was just 7, and too young to question any of it: the training sessions and the cultural dislocation; the two years spent away from her mother, Yelena, who was waiting for a visa to the United States; and the time in the academy dormitory with older girls as her father juggled jobs and a new language.

Other would-be champions have cracked in similar circumstances, discovering that they lacked the desire, the ability or the single-minded focus to keep swinging away. But Sharapova is not one to crack, and if there were any lingering doubts about her toughness or talent, she dispelled them in 1 hour 13 minutes with her 6-1, 6-4 victory in the final over Serena Williams.

Even before that, she had announced her intentions by winning the toss and electing to serve. She disappeared after the knock-up and those around the old place wondered if she was so consumed by nerves that she was finding it hard to prepare to play. But she won the first three points with stunning authority; she then won five straight games to take the opening set. But it was the manner in which she withstood two break points in the seventh game, when a break back might have given Williams fresh heart, that really stood out.

A break for Williams to lead 4-2 in the second set provided the youngster's first, and only, real moment of adversity the whole afternoon. She proved she had the mettle and, instead, it was the champion who looked edgy. Williams knew Sharapova was not

unravelling, either physically or mentally, and it was her forehand that failed.

To hold her own serve was imperative, and that Sharapova did was thanks, at 30-15, to a backhand lob of such wonderful aplomb and touch that Williams was applauding the ball in mid-flight. It is not often you see that.

At 4-4, Sharapova took a 40-15 lead on Williams's serve. But Williams, like her new rival, is not one to back down from a baseline fight. She saved the next two break points and would save one more. But Sharapova finally took a 5-4 lead after Williams slipped while moving forward to a short ball, then hooked a forehand wide. All that remained for Sharapova was the hardest part: serving for her first grand slam title. She missed a forehand at 40-15 on her first match point, but Williams was the one who missed the forehand on the last.

"She's kind of like me," Williams said, "she doesn't back off. She keeps giving it her all." Sharapova tossed her racket high into the air and sank to her knees at an improbable climax. "It's always been my dream to come here and to win," said Sharapova, the first Russian to ever win Wimbledon. "But it was never in my mind that I would do it this year.

"I have to take this away for one year; I'm sorry," Sharapova said to Serena as she held the gold-plated Venus Rosewater Dish. "I know there are going to be many more moments where we are going to play and I'm sure we're going to be here one more time and hopefully many more times."

Earlier in the day, at 10am, Julian Tatum, a member of the All England Club Management Committee, had offered a sneak peek at the member's badge burning a hole in his jacket pocket. It had the name Maria Sharapova on it, and this was five hours before the girl scorched her own page in tennis history and membership could be conferred. One of the glories of Wimbledon is that they never miss a trick.

Below: Maria Sharapova seems to know just how good she has become.
Bottom: Serena is grounded by a devastating Sharapova lob.

Top: Maria Sharapova embraces her father, whose sacrifices made her triumph possible.
Above: Serena Williams realises this won't be her year.
Left: Sharapova tries to phone her mother, who was watching back home in Russia.

Quote of the day

"To tell you the truth, I don't know what happened in the match, what my tactics were. I was just out there. I was in my own little world and I don't know what world really. When I saw the board with my name on it next to Wimbledon champion 2004, that was just it for me. "
Maria Sharapova

Shock of the day

A few tears were shed after Martina Navratilova (below) and Lisa Raymond lost in the semi-final of the doubles to Liezel Huber and Ai Sugiyama, thus bringing to an end the ambition of Navratilova seizing her record-breaking 21st Wimbledon title – at least for this year.

"Just the way it ended was real anti-climactic," Navratilova said as she and her partner digested a 7-6, 7-5 defeat. "Nerves got to me a little today, maybe not so much as in the past but if you don't get nervous, it means you don't care. It's how you deal with it. I tried hard yesterday, I tried hard the day before – that's probably the hardest I've ever tried and still lost. That's how it goes."

Sharapova was presented with her badge later in the evening and asked to pose for pictures on the member's balcony with it prominently pinned, the image of which will mark the front cover of the official Christmas cards sent out six months hence. The new champion did not think she was sufficiently well dressed for the shoot, so was driven back to her rented house for a change of frock. Then, carefully standing to one side so as to not show courts with covers on them behind her, smiled a gorgeous smile. And so she should. And so should women's tennis. Sharapova's extraordinary victory has radically altered the shape and texture of the women's game, which reacted to it with appropriately restrained delight.

The bosses cannot be seen to take sides; a win for Serena would have warmly endorsed a resurgence of her talents. But Sharapova's success, and its manner, has brought with her a sense of newness, a refreshing vitality that all sports need from time to time. That she is going to be a darling of the billboards and glossy magazines can't help but do tennis good as well.

"It is a defining moment for us," Larry Scott, the chief executive officer of the WTA, said. "We have seen the emergence of a new megastar for the sport and to have someone of such star power presented like Sharapova is very rare. I haven't seen anything like her since Boris Becker captured our imaginations in the mid-'80s. There is no doubt in my mind that there's room for her game to grow, which will only add a different dimension to the rivalries we've wanted to see at the top of the game. And I really think he is capable of transcending her nationality and the sport. I sat next to the president of NBC Sports [the US broadcasting company] during the final and he cannot wait for her to play in the United States."

To ease her development, the 17 year-old has been subject to an Age Eligibility rule that properly restricted the number of tournaments she could play – for instance at 16, only ten Tour events, plus Federation Cup and three exhibition, or non-Tour events were allowed. There had been times when Yuri, the father who used to carry his daughter on the handlebars of his bike, to practice at the Bollettieri Academy, argued

that Maria should be treated as a special case. Common sense prevailed and maybe a lot of other parents who might wish to push their offspring too quickly would be wise to accept the correctness of the rule. If she had played too much, too soon, would Sharapova be where she finds herself today? And there is now a sense that women's tennis has rediscovered its heart.

What the Williams sisters make of these diverse threats to their former domination is perhaps the most intriguing element of all. Once they were the chased, now they are the chasers. For the first time since 1999, neither Serena nor her older sister Venus held a grand slam singles title, and when the next rankings were issued two days later, Serena was 14th and Venus 15th, the first time in six years that neither was inside the top ten. As a foretaste, Roger Federer and Andy Roddick had duly won their semi-finals held over from the previous day. Federer was taken into a third set tie-break before defeating Sebastien Grosjean; Roddick dropped a set in ending Mario Ancic's brave run. The No.1 and No.2 men in the world would meet for the Wimbledon crown.

Above: Not all eyes were on Centre Court, as the Girls Singles semi-final encounter between Anna Inovic and Viktoria Azarenka attracts a sizeable gallery.

THE CHAMPIONSHIPS WIMBLEDON

SUNDAY 4 JULY

Day 13

Day 13 · Federer v Roddick

HE said he couldn't help himself. Roger Federer had sunk to his knees at the Royal Box end in 2003. This time he was looking right into the eyes of the royals lining the front row as he lashed in a 124mph ace out of reach of Andy Roddick's racquet and collapsed forwards. Federer's retention of his Wimbledon title left not a shred of doubt as to the qualities of the man.

At 22, Federer was the king of all he surveyed, a point that Tim Phillips, the Chairman of the Club would make at the Champions' Dinner at the Savoy Hotel later that evening. A final that started three times because of the dampness overhead was completed in a stunning shaft of sunlight – worthy acclaim for the man from Basel who performed at levels during the fortnight that had former champions struggling for words.

Boris Becker, the three-time champion, said: "This guy from Switzerland plays the kind of tennis I haven't seen anyone – and I mean anyone – reach before." John McEnroe, another legend of the championship, revered him as "quite simply one of the best, who could become the best ever."

As ever, Federer reflected with enormous modesty on the talents with which he had been bestowed. In a new twist to this wonderful day, the champion, who had defeated the No.2 seed 4-6, 7-6, 7-5, 6-4, was ushered onto the front steps of the All England Club to receive the adulation of the fans – most of whom had been kept in suspense by a day of grey, drizzle, more drizzle and, at the third time of its asking, a shaft of such brilliant sunlight that Roddick was all but dazzled by it.

Quote of The Championships

"I threw the kitchen sink at Roger
but he went to the bathroom and got
the tub."
Andy Roddick

Federer v Roddick • Day 13

If it had been Tim Henman out there receiving the runners-up applause, one doubts he would have received quite the ovation Roddick was afforded – and it had nothing to do with the special relationship on this, the day America hangs out the flags to celebrate freedom from British rule. Roddick had simply played a full part in defining this event. He had threatened to dismantle the finest game in the world and right at the end, his gasping determination to stay in the match received righteous acclaim.

The glory went to Federer. To win this once is magical; to come back and feel that gold again makes him double the player, double the champion, double the man. Last year, when he sobbed on television, he didn't like the fact so many pictures of him the next day concentrated solely on that image and so, 12 months on, he wept privately and it was over in a few seconds.

Tears of ecstasy in 2003 gave way to tears of utter relief in 2004; this had been a match won more on guts than glorious tennis, though there was plenty of that to satisfy all tastes, be they Swiss, American or neutral. How long will Roddick reflect on fighting back from 0-4 down in the second set to 4-4, to reach a point for the tie-break, before clobbering his otherwise majestic forehand way out of court and losing his serve for the third time in a set of five breaks?

How long will he reflect upon returning from the second rain break, leading 4-2 in the third set, sensing that if he were to pocket that, he would have one hand on the cup? Roddick had a point for a 5-3 lead but a net cord popped up an inviting forehand for Federer. The champion then fired a forehand service return at Roddick's feet, a forehand half-volley was steered wide and that opportunity went begging.

Federer won the first three games after that second re-start and after the first four points of the tie-break flashed by with aces and service winners, he produced a controlled backhand flicked shot from a dodgy bounce on the baseline, contriving to turn it into a winning pass. Roddick stood there, utterly aghast, either at his own misfortune or the opponent's brilliance. Probably combination of both. A sweeping backhand down the line

– the shot that Federer has improved beyond measure – secured him that set.

How long will Roddick reflect on the four break points in the fourth game of the fourth set – two of them forfeited to backhand returns he couldn't quite control. And what about the two further break points in the sixth game, a forehand slightly wide attempting an audacious pass, another into the net?

"I was taking it to him, I didn't want to get him into rallies, I was successful most of the time and on a couple of key points I wasn't and that was the match," Roddick said. "I wanted to give the first ball a ride and play the match on my terms. I'm growing more confident in my abilities, I do have a backhand and can hit it well. Volleying is an area where I can improve more and losses like this inspire me more and more. I feel like I'm on the right track. All is not lost because I lost today. I proved that Roger isn't quite invincible, but he's pretty close. I just came up short. We kill that term but today, it really was. But if you don't buy into Roger Federer now, you never will."

The Championships were positively festooned with ironies. One was that an event blighted by poor weather finished in lovely early-evening sunshine. Another was that mobile phones trilled repeatedly on Centre Court, even during the men's final, prompting umpires to deliver polite rebukes and all spectators except the shame-faced 'Nokia One' to erupt in supportive applause. Yet on the only occasion when everyone on the court actually urged a mobile to burst into action, as young Maria Sharapova tried to phone her mother in Florida following her remarkable victory in Saturday's final, she couldn't get a signal.

Another irony was that had Roddick defeated Federer, it would have been considered by some tennis cognoscenti to be an even greater shock than Sharapova's defeat of Serena Williams. Yet Roddick was the No.2 seed, with the fastest serve in the world, and shortly before The Championships had reminded everyone of his ability on grass by successfully defending his title at Queen's. How could a victory for such a marvellous player possibly

Opposite: Roger Federer kisses the coveted trophy.

Day 13

Opposite: Woodbridge and Bjorkman celebrate another doubles triumph.
Below: Rennae Stubbs and Cara Black were victorious in the Ladies Doubles.

have been considered an upset? Quite simply, because he was playing Federer.

The remarkable Todd Woodbridge of Australia won his ninth men's doubles title, the first six of which had been with his old partner Mark Woodforde and now, for a third year in succession, with Jonas Bjorkman of Sweden. Woodbridge beat the record of eight that had been held by British brothers, Laurie and Reggie Doherty at the turn of the 20th Century. At the end of their 6-1, 6-4, 4-6, 6-4 victory over the unseeded pair, Julian Knowle of Austria and Nenad Zimobjic of Serbia and Montenegro, Woodbridge held nine fingers to the corners of the court, a look of disbelief on his face. "Geez, I'm proud of that performance," Woodbridge said, "and I believe some of my shots are better than they were ten years ago. I certainly serve way better."

There was much riotous celebration in the Black family from Zimbabwe. Cara, the 25 year-old younger sister of Byron, now retired, and Wayne, had woken early knowing that she had the possibility of winning two Wimbledon titles. It needed three matches to achieve a double dream but at the end of a day when she was close to exhaustion, everything came right.

Cara and Rennae Stubbs from Australia defeated Ai Sugiyama of Japan and Liezel Huber from South Africa, Black finishing off the victory with a smash. Then she and Wayne returned to defeat Todd Woodbridge – who had had quite a day himself – and Alicia Molik of Australia, saving match points in the process. "I've won a doubles title at the French but what I've been able to do means more because Wimbledon always meant so

much to my Dad, Don, who passed away four years ago," Cara said. "It was Dad who got me and my brothers playing tennis and the thing that inspired us was to win Wimbledon one day. I couldn't be happier."

At 8.30pm on Sunday evening it was all over. The Blacks were the last to arrive for The Champions' Dinner but no one minded in the least. The speeches didn't start until 1am on Monday morning and no one minded that either.

The juniors had all stayed awake. Gael Monfils of France defeated Britain's Miles Kasiri 7-5, 7-6 to take the boy's title, and continue a run that had seen him win both the Australian and French crowns. Only Sweden's Stefan Edberg, in 1983, had previously completed a grand slam of the junior championships. Kasiri had more than enough compensation in being the first Briton in the final of the boys since Buster Mottram in 1972.

The No.6 seed Katerina Bondarenko of Ukraine won the girls' title, defeating Ana Ivanovic from Serbia and Montenegro 6-4, 6-7, 6-2 in a splendid final. A team from Belarus – whose men had reached the Davis Cup semi-finals for the first time this year – won the girls' doubles: Viktoria Azarenka (at only 14 years-old) and Volha Havartsova beating the pair of Marina Erakovic of New Zealand and Monica Niculescu of Romania 6-4, 3-6, 6-4.

The boys' doubles title went to the American pair Brendan Evans and Scott Oudsema, who beat Robin Haase of the Netherlands and Victor Troicki of Serbia and Montenegro 6-4, 6-4.

In the golden oldies, Jana Novotna, the 1998 ladies singles champion, teamed up with Mima Jausovec to beat Jo Durie and Helena Sukova 1-6, 7-5, 6-1 in the Invitational over-35s; while the Americans TJ Middleton and David Wheaton lifted the men's over-35s title, defeating their compatriot Robert Seguso and Frenchman, Cedric Pioline.

Kevin Curren and Johan Kriek, two native South Africans, won the Over-45 mens' title, with a 4-6, 6-1, 6-4 win over Heinz Guenthardt and Balazs Taroczy. During one of the rain breaks, it was wonderful to see Curren chatting animatedly with Boris Becker, who had defeated him in that unforgettable 1985 men's final. Friends linked forever through a great sport and its greatest championship.

Above: Girls Singles Champion, Katerina Bondarenko.
Left: Boys Singles Runner-Up, Britain's Miles Kasiri.
Centre left: Girls Singles Runner-Up Ana Ivanovic.
Far left: Boys Singles Champion, Gael Monfils.

The Ladies' Singles Championship

Maria Sharapova

The Gentlemen's Doubles Championship

Todd Woodbridge & Jonas Bjorkman

The Mixed Doubles Championship

Wayne Black & Cara Black

The Gentlemen's Singles Championship

Roger Federer

The Ladies' Doubles Championship

Cara Black & Rennae Stubbs

The 35 and over Ladies' Invitation Doubles

Mima Jausovec & Jana Novotna

The Girls' Doubles Championship

Viktoria Azarenka & Volha Havartsova

The Boys' Singles Championship

Gael Monfils

The Boys' Doubles Championship

Brendon Evans & Scott Oudsema

The Girls' Singles Championship

Katerina Bondarenko

The 35 and over Gentlemens' Invitation Doubles

T-J Middleton & David Wheaton

The 45 and over Gentlemen's Invitation Doubles

Johan Kriek & Kevin Curren

CHAMPIONSHIP RECORDS 2004

ALPHABETICAL LIST OF COMPETITORS

LADIES

- Ani Miss M. *(Estonia)*
- **39** Asagoe Miss S. *(Japan)*
- **102** Ashley Miss T. *(USA)*
- Bacheva Miss L. *(Bulgaria)*
- Baker Miss L. *(New Zealand)*
- **30** Baltacha Miss E. *(Great Britain)*
- **108** Barna Miss A. *(Germany)*
- **106** Bartoli Miss M. *(France)*
- **124** Beltrame Miss S. *(France)*
- **68** Benesova Miss I. *(Czech Republic)*
- **114** Beygelzimer Miss Y. *(Ukraine)*
- **78** Birnerova Miss E. *(Czech Republic)*
- **86** Black Miss C. *(Zimbabwe)*
- Blahotova Miss O. *(Czech Republic)*
- Borwell Miss S. *(Great Britain)*
- **120** Bovina Miss E. *(Russia)*
- **67** Brandi Miss K. *(Puerto Rico)*
- **52** Callens Miss E.S.H. *(Belgium)*
- **107** Camerin Miss M. *(Italy)*
- **32** Capriati Miss J. *(USA)*
- Cargill Miss A. *(USA)*
- **10** Casanova Miss M. *(Switzerland)*
- **75** Castano Miss C. *(Colombia)*
- **38** Cervanova Miss L. *(Slovak Republic)*
- **84** Chladkova Miss D. *(Czech Republic)*
- Cho Miss Y.J. *(Korea Republic)*
- **4** Cohen-Aloro Miss S. *(France)*
- Collin Miss H. *(Great Britain)*
- **85** Craybas Miss J. *(USA)*
- Crook Miss H. *(Great Britain)*
- **103** Czink Miss M. *(Hungary)*
- **8** Daniilidou Miss E. *(Greece)*
- **65** Davenport Miss L. *(USA)*
- **25** Dechy Miss N. *(France)*
- **97** Dementieva Miss E. *(Russia)*
- Dhenin Miss C. *(France)*
- **73** Dokic Miss J. *(Serbia and Montenegro)*
- Dominikovic Miss E. *(Australia)*
- **87** Douchevina Miss V. *(Russia)*
- **74** Dulko Miss G. *(Argentina)*
- **48** Farina Elia Mrs S. *(Italy)*
- **3** Foretz Miss S. *(France)*
- **121** Frazier Miss A. *(USA)*
- Fujiwara Miss R. *(Japan)*
- **13** Gagliardi Miss E. *(Switzerland)*
- **119** Gallovits Miss E. *(Romania)*
- **54** Garbin Miss T. *(Italy)*
- **11** Golovin Miss T. *(France)*
- **59** Grande Miss R. *(Italy)*
- **94** Granville Miss L. *(USA)*
- **99** Groenefeld Miss A. *(Germany)*
- Gubacsi Miss Z. *(Hungary)*
- **117** Hantuchova Miss D. *(Slovak Republic)*
- **51** Harkleroad Miss A. *(USA)*
- Hawkins Miss A. *(Great Britain)*
- **36** Hopkins Miss J. *(USA)*
- Huber Mrs L. *(South Africa)*
- Husarova Miss J. *(Slovak Republic)*
- **90** Irvin Miss M. *(USA)*
- **111** Janes Miss A. *(Great Britain)*
- **109** Jankovic Miss J. *(Serbia and Montenegro)*
- Jeon Miss M-R. *(Korea Republic)*
- **12** Jidkova Miss A. *(Russia)*
- **125** Jugic-Salkic Miss M. *(Bosnia-Herzegovina)*
- Jurak Miss D. *(Croatia)*
- **126** Kapros Miss A. *(Hungary)*
- **115** Keothavong Miss A. *(Great Britain)*
- **122** Kirilenko Miss M. *(Russia)*
- **98** Kleinova Miss S. *(Czech Republic)*
- **34** Kostanic Miss J. *(Croatia)*
- **110** Koukalova Miss K. *(Czech Republic)*
- **43** Krasnoroutskaya Miss L. *(Russia)*
- **55** Kremer Miss A. *(Luxembourg)*
- Krizan Miss T. *(Slovenia)*
- Kulikovskaya Miss E. *(Russia)*
- **127** Kurhajcova Miss L. *(Slovak Republic)*
- **64** Kuznetsova Miss S. *(Russia)*
- Lee Miss J. *(Chinese Taipei)*
- **5** Lee-Waters Mrs L. *(USA)*
- Lehnhoff Miss J. *(USA)*
- **61** Leon Garcia Miss G. *(Spain)*
- Li Miss T. *(China P.R.)*
- Liggan Miss K. *(Ireland)*
- **62** Likhovtseva Miss E. *(Russia)*
- **92** Llagostera Vives Miss N. *(Spain)*
- **72** Loit Miss E. *(France)*
- **88** Maleeva Miss M. *(Bulgaria)*
- **91** Mandula Miss P. *(Hungary)*
- **29** Marrero Miss M. *(Spain)*
- **24** Martinez Miss C. *(Spain)*
- Mattek Miss B. *(USA)*
- **33** Mauresmo Miss A. *(France)*
- McShea Miss L. *(Australia)*
- **26** Medina Garrigues Miss A. *(Spain)*
- **95** Mikaelian Miss M-G. *(Switzerland)*
- Miyagi Miss N. *(Japan)*
- **104** Molik Miss A. *(Australia)*
- **15** Morigami Miss A. *(Japan)*
- **128** Myskina Miss A. *(Russia)*
- Nagy Miss K. *(Hungary)*
- **44** Nagyova Miss H. *(Slovak Republic)*
- Navratilova Miss G. *(Czech Republic)*
- **76** Navratilova Miss M. *(USA)*
- **28** O'Brien Miss K. *(Great Britain)*
- **6** O'Donoghue Miss J. *(Great Britain)*
- **77** Obata Miss S. *(Japan)*
- **71** Panova Miss T. *(Russia)*
- **58** Parra Santonja Miss A. *(Spain)*
- Pastikova Miss M. *(Czech Republic)*
- **47** Peng Miss S. *(China P.R.)*
- **18** Pennetta Miss F. *(Italy)*
- **21** Perebiynis Miss T. *(Ukraine)*
- **50** Perry Miss S. *(USA)*
- **17** Petrova Miss N. *(Russia)*
- **41** Pierce Miss M. *(France)*
- **101** Pisnik Miss T. *(Slovenia)*
- Poutchek Miss T. *(Belarus)*
- Prakusya Miss W. *(Indonesia)*
- **116** Pratt Miss N.J. *(Australia)*
- Prusova Miss L. *(Czech Republic)*
- **66** Randriantefy Miss D. *(Madagascar)*
- **40** Raymond Miss L.M. *(USA)*
- **63** Razzano Miss V. *(France)*
- **118** Reeves Miss S. *(USA)*
- Rittner Miss B. *(Germany)*
- Rodionova Miss A. *(Russia)*
- **42** Ruano Pascual Miss V. *(Spain)*
- **105** Rubin Miss C. *(USA)*
- Russell Miss J. *(USA)*
- **57** Safina Miss D. *(Russia)*
- **27** Sanchez Lorenzo Miss M. *(Spain)*
- Sanchez Vicario Miss A. *(Spain)*
- **60** Santangelo Miss M. *(Italy)*
- **31** Schaul Miss C. *(Luxembourg)*
- **37** Schett Miss B. *(Austria)*
- **9** Schiavone Miss F. *(Italy)*
- **16** Schnyder Miss P. *(Switzerland)*
- **23** Sequera Miss M. *(Venezuela)*
- **7** Serna Miss M. *(Spain)*
- Serra Zanetti Miss A. *(Italy)*
- Serra Zanetti Miss A. *(Italy)*
- Sewell Miss N. *(Australia)*
- **113** Sharapova Miss M. *(Russia)*
- **89** Shaughnessy Miss M. *(USA)*
- **81** Smashnova-Pistolesi Mrs A. *(Israel)*
- **14** Snyder Miss T. *(USA)*
- Spears Miss A. *(USA)*
- **93** Sprem Miss K. *(Croatia)*
- **82** Srebotnik Miss K. *(Slovenia)*
- Stewart Miss B. *(Australia)*
- **79** Stosur Miss S. *(Australia)*
- **45** Strycova Miss B. *(Czech Republic)*
- Stubbs Miss R.P. *(Australia)*
- **49** Suarez Miss P. *(Argentina)*
- **19** Sucha Miss M. *(Slovak Republic)*
- **112** Sugiyama Miss A. *(Japan)*
- **53** Sun Miss T.T. *(China P.R.)*
- Svensson Mrs A. *(Sweden)*
- **46** Talaja Miss S. *(Croatia)*
- **100** Tanasugarn Miss T. *(Thailand)*
- Tarabini Miss P. *(Argentina)*
- Tatarkova Miss E. *(Ukraine)*
- Tu Miss M. *(USA)*
- **35** Vakulenko Miss J. *(Ukraine)*
- **20** Vento-Kabchi Mrs M. *(Venezuela)*
- Vinci Miss R. *(Italy)*
- Wartusch Miss P. *(Austria)*
- **70** Washington Miss M. *(USA)*
- **123** Webley-Smith Miss E. *(Great Britain)*
- **83** Weingartner Miss M. *(Germany)*
- **22** Wheeler Miss C. *(Australia)*
- **69** Widjaja Miss A. *(Indonesia)*
- **1** Williams Miss S. *(USA)*
- **96** Williams Miss V. *(USA)*
- Yan Miss Z. *(China P.R.)*
- Yoshida Miss Y. *(Japan)*
- **2** Zheng Miss J. *(China P.R.)*
- **56** Zuluaga Miss F. *(Colombia)*
- **80** Zvonareva Miss V. *(Russia)*

GENTLEMEN

- **62** Acasuso J. *(Argentina)*
- Allegro Y. *(Switzerland)*
- **95** Ancic M. *(Croatia)*
- **75** Andreev I. *(Russia)*
- **72** Arazi H. *(Morocco)*
- Arnold L. *(Argentina)*
- **36** Arthurs W. *(Australia)*
- **50** Ascione T. *(France)*
- Aspelin S. *(Sweden)*
- Auckland J. *(Great Britain)*
- Bachelot J-F. *(France)*
- Banks A. *(Great Britain)*
- **85** Beck K. *(Slovak Republic)*
- **93** Benneteau J. *(France)*
- **94** Berdych T. *(Czech Republic)*
- Bertolini M. *(Italy)*
- Bhupathi M. *(India)*
- **41** Bjorkman J. *(Sweden)*
- Black W. *(Zimbabwe)*
- **108** Blanco G. *(Spain)*
- **10** Bloomfield R. *(Great Britain)*
- **2** Bogdanovic A. *(Great Britain)*
- **63** Boutter J. *(France)*
- Bowen D. *(USA)*
- Braasch K. *(Germany)*
- **53** Bracciali D. *(Italy)*
- Browne F. *(Argentina)*
- Bryan B. *(USA)*
- Bryan M. *(USA)*
- **106** Burgsmuller L. *(Germany)*
- **110** Canas G. *(Argentina)*
- **117** Carlsen K. *(Denmark)*
- Carrasco J. *(Spain)*
- **52** Carraz G. *(France)*
- Cermak F. *(Czech Republic)*
- **105** Chela J.I. *(Argentina)*
- **111** Childs L. *(Great Britain)*
- Cibulec T. *(Czech Republic)*
- **45** Clement A. *(France)*
- Coetzee J. *(South Africa)*
- **33** Coria G. *(Argentina)*
- **19** Corretja A. *(Spain)*
- **92** Costa A. *(Spain)*
- Damm M. *(Czech Republic)*
- **78** Davydenko N. *(Russia)*
- De Voest R. *(South Africa)*
- **27** Delgado J. *(Great Britain)*
- **122** Delgado R. *(Paraguay)*
- **121** Dent T. *(USA)*
- **83** Dupuis A. *(France)*
- Eagle J. *(Australia)*
- **13** Elseneer G. *(Belgium)*
- **107** Enqvist T. *(Sweden)*
- Erlich J. *(Israel)*
- Etlis G. *(Argentina)*
- **4** Falla A. *(Colombia)*
- **1** Federer R. *(Switzerland)*
- **39** Ferreira W. *(South Africa)*
- **69** Ferrer D. *(Spain)*
- **64** Ferrero J.C. *(Spain)*
- **48** Fish M. *(USA)*
- Fisher A. *(Australia)*
- Flanagan I. *(Great Britain)*
- Friedl L. *(Czech Republic)*
- Fyrstenberg M. *(Poland)*
- Galimberti G. *(Italy)*
- **55** Gambill J-M. *(USA)*
- Garcia M. *(Argentina)*
- **118** Gasquet R. *(France)*
- Gimelstob J. *(USA)*
- **57** Ginepri R. *(USA)*
- **73** Gonzalez F. *(Chile)*
- **49** Grosjean S. *(France)*
- **84** Haas T. *(Germany)*
- Haggard C. *(South Africa)*
- **70** Hanescu V. *(Romania)*
- Hanley P. *(Australia)*
- Healey N. *(Australia)*
- **65** Henman T. *(Great Britain)*
- **38** Hernandez O. *(Spain)*
- **54** Hernych J. *(Czech Republic)*
- **68** Heuberger I. *(Switzerland)*
- **32** Hewitt L. *(Australia)*
- Hill M. *(Australia)*
- **91** Hilton M.A. *(Great Britain)*
- Hood M. *(Argentina)*
- **96** Horna L. *(Peru)*
- **89** Hrbaty D. *(Slovak Republic)*
- Humphries S. *(USA)*
- Huss S. *(Australia)*
- **26** Ivanisevic G. *(Croatia)*
- **46** Johansson J. *(Sweden)*
- **7** Johansson T. *(Sweden)*
- **15** Karlovic I. *(Croatia)*
- Kerr J. *(Australia)*
- **8** Kiefer N. *(Germany)*
- Kiernan D. *(Great Britain)*
- Kisgyorgy G. *(Hungary)*
- **3** Knowle J. *(Austria)*
- Knowles M. *(Bahamas)*
- Koenig R. *(South Africa)*
- Kohlmann M. *(Germany)*
- **61** Koubek S. *(Austria)*
- Kubot L. *(Poland)*
- **37** Kucera K. *(Slovak Republic)*
- **29** Labadze I. *(Georgia)*
- Landsberg J. *(Sweden)*
- Leach R. *(USA)*
- Lee M. *(Great Britain)*
- Levinsky J. *(Czech Republic)*
- Lindstedt R. *(Sweden)*
- **40** Ljubicic I. *(Croatia)*
- **12** Llodra M. *(France)*
- **9** Lopez F. *(Spain)*
- **22** Lopez M. *(Spain)*
- Lopez Moron A. *(Spain)*
- **44** Lu Y. *(Chinese Taipei)*
- MacPhie B. *(USA)*
- Mahut N. *(France)*
- **82** Malisse X. *(Belgium)*
- **101** Mantilla F. *(Spain)*
- **86** Marray J. *(Great Britain)*
- **5** Martin A. *(Spain)*
- **109** Martin T. *(USA)*
- **113** Massu N. *(Chile)*
- Matkowski M. *(Poland)*
- **35** Mayer F. *(Germany)*
- **31** Melzer J. *(Austria)*
- Merklein M. *(Bahamas)*
- **56** Mirnyi M. *(Belarus)*
- **116** Montanes A. *(Spain)*
- **34** Moodie W. *(South Africa)*
- **17** Moya C. *(Spain)*
- **47** Navarro Pastor I. *(Spain)*
- Nestor D. *(Canada)*
- **81** Novak J. *(Czech Republic)*
- Oliver G. *(USA)*
- Paes L. *(India)*
- Pala P. *(Czech Republic)*
- Palmer J. *(USA)*
- **14** Parmar A. *(Great Britain)*
- Parrott T. *(USA)*
- **18** Patience O. *(France)*
- **120** Pavel A. *(Romania)*
- Perry T. *(Australia)*
- **123** Pescosolido S. *(Italy)*
- **125** Peya A. *(Austria)*
- **80** Philippoussis M. *(Australia)*
- Phillips T. *(USA)*
- **102** Pless K. *(Denmark)*
- **114** Popp A. *(Germany)*
- Prieto S. *(Argentina)*
- **119** Ram A. *(Israel)*
- **66** Ramirez Hidalgo R. *(Spain)*
- **103** Reid T. *(Australia)*
- Rikl D. *(Czech Republic)*
- **88** Robredo T. *(Spain)*
- **79** Rochus C. *(Belgium)*
- **51** Rochus O. *(Belgium)*
- **128** Roddick A. *(USA)*
- Rodriguez M. *(Argentina)*
- **99** Rusedski G. *(Great Britain)*
- **71** Sa A. *(Brazil)*
- **24** Safin M. *(Russia)*
- **126** Salzenstein J. *(USA)*
- **90** Sanchez D. *(Spain)*
- **100** Sanguinetti D. *(Italy)*
- **6** Santoro F. *(France)*
- **67** Saretta F. *(Brazil)*
- **21** Sargsian S. *(Armenia)*
- **11** Saulnier C. *(France)*
- **112** Schalken S. *(Netherlands)*
- **97** Schuettler R. *(Germany)*
- Sherwood D. *(Great Britain)*
- Skoch D. *(Czech Republic)*
- **42** Sluiter R. *(Netherlands)*
- **98** Soderling R. *(Sweden)*
- **104** Spadea V. *(USA)*
- **16** Srichaphan P. *(Thailand)*
- **87** Starace P. *(Italy)*
- **20** Stepanek R. *(Czech Republic)*
- Suk C. *(Czech Republic)*
- Thomas J. *(USA)*
- **58** Tipsarevic J. *(Serbia and Montenegro)*
- **23** Tursunov D. *(Russia)*
- **115** Ulihrach B. *(Czech Republic)*
- Ullyett K. *(Zimbabwe)*
- **43** Vacek J. *(Czech Republic)*
- **76** Van Lottum J. *(Netherlands)*
- **124** Van Scheppingen D. *(Netherlands)*
- Vanhoudt T. *(Belgium)*
- **74** Vassallo Arguello M. *(Italy)*
- **59** Verdasco F. *(Spain)*
- **77** Verkerk M. *(Netherlands)*
- Vizner P. *(Czech Republic)*
- **30** Vliegen K. *(Belgium)*
- **28** Volandri F. *(Italy)*
- **127** Wang Y-T. *(Chinese Taipei)*
- Wassen R. *(Netherlands)*
- **60** Weiner G. *(USA)*
- Woodbridge T.A. *(Australia)*
- **25** Youzhny M. *(Russia)*
- Zimonjic N. *(Serbia and Montenegro)*

GIRLS

- Ancic Miss S. *(Croatia)*
- Azarenka Miss V. *(Belarus)*
- Balda Miss E. *(Ecuador)*
- Biglmaier Miss M. *(Germany)*
- Bondarenko Miss K. *(Ukraine)*
- Chan Miss Y-J. *(Chinese Taipei)*
- Chvojkova Miss V. *(Czech Republic)*
- Cohen Miss J. *(USA)*
- Erakovic Miss M. *(New Zealand)*
- Ferguson Miss S. *(Australia)*
- Frankova Miss N. *(Czech Republic)*
- Fuda Miss R. *(Japan)*
- Gabba Miss G. *(Italy)*
- Gajdosova Miss J. *(Slovak Republic)*
- Gojnea Miss M. *(Romania)*
- Grady Miss H. *(Great Britain)*
- Grebeniuk Miss E. *(Russia)*
- Gullickson Miss C. *(USA)*
- Havartsova Miss V. *(Belarus)*
- Hsu Miss W-H. *(Chinese Taipei)*
- Ivanovic Miss A. *(Serbia and Montenegro)*
- Jerman Miss A. *(Slovenia)*
- Juricova Miss J. *(Slovak Republic)*
- Kerber Miss A. *(Germany)*
- Kirkland Miss J. *(USA)*
- Kleybanova Miss A. *(Russia)*
- Kosminskaya Miss E. *(Russia)*
- Kotkina Miss I. *(Russia)*
- Krajicek Miss M. *(Netherlands)*
- Kramperova Miss K. *(Czech Republic)*
- Kudryavtseva Miss A. *(Russia)*
- Lukic Miss V. *(Serbia and Montenegro)*
- Malek Miss T. *(Germany)*
- Marcio Miss K. *(USA)*
- Niculescu Miss M. *(Romania)*
- O'Brien Miss K. *(Great Britain)*
- Peer Miss S. *(Israel)*
- Peterzan Miss C. *(Great Britain)*
- Rodina Miss E. *(Russia)*
- Rybarikova Miss M. *(Slovak Republic)*
- Schnack Miss Y. *(USA)*
- Schutte Miss G. *(South Africa)*
- South Miss M. *(Great Britain)*
- Sun Miss S-N. *(China P.R.)*
- Szatmari Miss A. *(Romania)*
- Szavay Miss A. *(Hungary)*
- Thongdach Miss P. *(Thailand)*
- Vaidisova Miss N. *(Czech Republic)*
- Verardi Miss V. *(Italy)*
- Vesnina Miss E. *(Russia)*
- Wozniak Miss A. *(Canada)*
- Zec-Peskiric Miss M. *(Slovenia)*

BOYS

- Alcaide-Justell G. *(Spain)*
- Amado J.P. *(Argentina)*
- Andujar-Alba P. *(Spain)*
- Arevalo Gonzalez R. *(El Salvador)*
- Arnaboldi A. *(Italy)*
- Baker J. *(Great Britain)*
- Bellucci T. *(Brazil)*
- Bubka S. *(Ukraine)*
- Capkovic K. *(Slovak Republic)*
- Cavaday N. *(Great Britain)*
- De Rijke R. *(Netherlands)*
- Del Potro J-M. *(Argentina)*
- Evans B. *(USA)*
- Ferguson L. *(Australia)*
- Fognini F. *(Italy)*
- Haase R. *(Netherlands)*
- Jenkins S. *(USA)*
- Jones G.D. *(New Zealand)*
- Jun W-S. *(Korea Republic)*
- Kasiri M. *(Great Britain)*
- Kerley J. *(Australia)*
- Kim S-Y. *(Korea Republic)*
- Kuznetsov A. *(USA)*
- Lacko L. *(Slovak Republic)*
- Liberhan T. *(India)*
- Miklusicak P. *(Slovak Republic)*
- Mirzadeh V. *(USA)*
- Monfils G. *(France)*
- Muller D. *(Germany)*
- Murray A. *(Great Britain)*
- Murray J. *(Great Britain)*
- Nedovesov A. *(Ukraine)*
- Neilly T. *(USA)*
- Ouanna J. *(France)*
- Oudsema S. *(USA)*
- Rastogi K. *(India)*
- Rieschick S. *(Germany)*
- Rushby T. *(Great Britain)*
- Schwank E. *(Argentina)*
- Sharan D. *(India)*
- Simmonds P. *(USA)*
- Troicki V. *(Serbia and Montenegro)*
- Van Keulen C. *(Netherlands)*
- Visak V. *(Croatia)*
- Ward W. *(New Zealand)*
- Wire R. *(Great Britain)*
- Wolmarans F. *(South Africa)*
- Yi C-H. *(Chinese Taipei)*
- Young D. *(USA)*
- Ziadi M. *(Morocco)*
- Zverev M. *(Germany)*

Bold figures denote position in Singles Draw

THE GENTLEMEN'S SINGLES CHAMPIONSHIP

Holder: R Federer

The winner becomes the holder, for the year only, of the CHALLENGE CUP presented by The All England Lawn Tennis and Croquet Club. The winner receives a silver replica of the Challenge Cup. A silver salver is presented to the runner-up and a bronze medal to each defeated semi-finalist.

First Round

1. **Federer, Roger [1] *(1)*** ....(SUI)
(W) 2. Bogdanovic, Alex *(295)*.................(GBR)
(Q) 3. Knowle, Julian *(209)* ....(AUT)
(Q) 4. Falla, Alejandro *(138)*....................(COL)
5. Martin, Alberto *(61)* ....(ESP)
6. Santoro, Fabrice *(53)*.......................(FRA)
7. Johansson, Thomas *(23pr)* ....(SWE)
8. **Kiefer, Nicolas [29] *(33)*** ....(GER)
9. **Lopez, Feliciano [18] *(22)*** ....(ESP)
(W) 10. Bloomfield, Richard *(529)*.............(GBR)
11. Saulnier, Cyril *(83)* ....(FRA)
12. Llodra, Michael *(50)* ....(FRA)
13. Elseneer, Gilles *(99)*........................(BEL)
(W) 14. Parmar, Arvind *(162)* ....(GBR)
15. Karlovic, Ivo *(62)* ....(CRO)
16. **Srichaphan, Paradorn [13] *(14)*** .....(THA)
17. **Moya, Carlos [9] *(7)***........................(ESP)
(Q) 18. Patience, Olivier *(93)* ....(FRA)
19. Corretja, Alex *(85)* ....(ESP)
20. Stepanek, Radek *(67)* ....(CZE)
21. Sargsian, Sargis *(48)* ....(ARM)
22. Lopez, Marc *(120)* ....(ESP)
23. Tursunov, Dmitry *(70)*.....................(RUS)
24. **Safin, Marat [19] *(15)*** ....(RUS)
25. **Youzhny, Mikhail [31] *(35)*** ....(RUS)
26. Ivanisevic, Goran *(17pr)* ....(CRO)
(Q) 27. Delgado, Jamie *(301)* ....(GBR)
28. Volandri, Filippo *(52)* ....(ITA)
29. Labadze, Irakli *(45)*.........................(GEO)
30. Vliegen, Kristof *(107)*......................(BEL)
31. Melzer, Jurgen *(42)*.........................(AUT)
32. **Hewitt, Lleyton [7] *(10)***.................(AUS)
33. **Coria, Guillermo [3] *(3)***................(ARG)
34. Moodie, Wesley *(106)* ....(RSA)
35. Mayer, Florian *(66)* ....(GER)
36. Arthurs, Wayne *(96)* ....(AUS)
37. Kucera, Karol *(76)*...........................(SVK)
38. Hernandez, Oscar *(88)* ....(ESP)
39. Ferreira, Wayne *(82)* ....(RSA)
40. **Ljubicic, Ivan [28] *(29)*** ....(CRO)
41. **Bjorkman, Jonas [17] *(27)*** ....(SWE)
42. Sluiter, Raemon *(79)* ....(NED)
43. Vacek, Jan *(133)* ....(CZE)
44. Lu, Yen-Hsun *(101)*.........................(TPE)
45. Clement, Arnaud *(47)* ....(FRA)
46. Johansson, Joachim *(43)*.................(SWE)
(Q) 47. Navarro Pastor, Ivan *(228)*...............(ESP)
48. **Fish, Mardy [14] *(20)***......................(USA)
49. **Grosjean, Sebastien [10] *(13)***.........(FRA)
50. Ascione, Thierry *(86)*.......................(FRA)
51. Rochus, Olivier *(74)* ....(BEL)
52. Carraz, Gregory *(69)*.......................(FRA)
(Q) 53. Bracciali, Daniele *(218)* ....(ITA)
(Q) 54. Hernych, Jan *(118)*..........................(CZE)
55. Gambill, Jan-Michael *(84)* ....(USA)
56. **Mirnyi, Max [23] *(28)***......................(BLR)
57. **Ginepri, Robby [27] *(34)*** ....(USA)
(Q) 58. Tipsarevic, Janko *(136)* ....(SCG)
59. Verdasco, Fernando *(40)*.................(ESP)
(Q) 60. Weiner, Glenn *(141)* ....(USA)
61. Koubek, Stefan *(95)*........................(AUT)
62. Acasuso, Jose *(97)*..........................(ARG)
63. Boutter, Julien *(100pr)*....................(FRA)
64. **Ferrero, Juan Carlos [6] *(5)***............(ESP)
65. **Henman, Tim [5] *(6)***.......................(GBR)
66. Ramirez Hidalgo, Ruben *(89)* ....(ESP)
67. Saretta, Flavio *(68)* ....(BRA)
(Q) 68. Heuberger, Ivo *(137)*........................(SUI)
69. Ferrer, David *(49)*............................(ESP)
70. Hanescu, Victor *(75)* ....(ROM)
(Q) 71. Sa, Andre *(255)* ....(BRA)
72. **Arazi, Hicham [32] *(39)*** ....(MAR)
73. **Gonzalez, Fernando [24] *(26)*** ....(CHI)
74. Vassallo Arguello, Martin *(108)*.......(ITA)
75. Andreev, Igor *(64)*..........................(RUS)
76. Van Lottum, John *(115)*...................(NED)
77. Verkerk, Martin *(56)*.......................(NED)
78. Davydenko, Nikolay *(59)* ....(RUS)
(Q) 79. Rochus, Christophe *(122)* ....(BEL)
80. **Philippoussis, Mark [11] *(17)***.........(AUS)
81. **Novak, Jiri [16] *(16)***.......................(CZE)
82. Malisse, Xavier *(51)*........................(BEL)
83. Dupuis, Antony *(92)* ....(FRA)
84. Haas, Tommy *(11pr)* ....(GER)
85. Beck, Karol *(71)*.............................(SVK)
(W) 86. Marray, Jonathan *(238)*..................(GBR)
(L) 87. Starace, Potito *(131)*.........................(ITA)
88. **Robredo, Tommy [20] *(19)*** ....(ESP)
89. **Hrbaty, Dominik [25] *(25)*** ....(SVK)
90. Sanchez, David *(54)* ....(ESP)
(W) 91. Hilton, Mark *(479)*...........................(GBR)
92. Costa, Albert *(55)*............................(ESP)
(L) 93. Benneteau, Julien *(80)* ....(FRA)
94. Berdych, Tomas *(65)* ....(CZE)
95. Ancic, Mario *(63)* ....(CRO)
96. **Horna, Luis [33] *(36)***......................(PER)
97. **Schuettler, Rainer [8] *(8)*** ....(GER)
98. Soderling, Robin *(37)* ....(SWE)
(W) 99. Rusedski, Greg *(165)*.......................(GBR)
(L) 100. Sanguinetti, Davide *(112)*................(ITA)
101. Mantilla, Felix *(127)* ....(ESP)
102. Pless, Kristian *(104pr)* ....(DEN)
(W) 103. Reid, Todd *(134)*...........................(AUS)
104. **Spadea, Vincent [30] *(30)*** ....(USA)
105. **Chela, Juan Ignacio [21] *(18)***........(ARG)
106. Burgsmuller, Lars *(94)*....................(GER)
107. Enqvist, Thomas *(57)* ....(SWE)
108. Blanco, Galo *(102)*..........................(ESP)
109. Martin, Todd *(72)* ....(USA)
110. Canas, Guillermo *(73)* ....(ARG)
(W) 111. Childs, Lee *(251)*............................(GBR)
112. **Schalken, Sjeng [12] *(23)*** ....(NED)
113. **Massu, Nicolas [15] *(12)*** ....(CHI)
114. Popp, Alexander *(90)*.....................(GER)
115. Ulihrach, Bohdan *(79pr)*.................(CZE)
116. Montanes, Albert *(78)*.....................(ESP)
117. Carlsen, Kenneth *(103)* ....(DEN)
(Q) 118. Gasquet, Richard *(105)*...................(FRA)
(Q) 119. Ram, Andy *(364)* ....(ISR)
120. **Pavel, Andrei [22] *(21)*** ....(ROM)
121. **Dent, Taylor [26] *(31)***......................(USA)
(Q) 122. Delgado, Ramon *(200)* ....(PAR)
(L) 123. Pescosolido, Stefano *(143)* ....(ITA)
124. Van Scheppingen, Dennis *(87)*......(NED)
(L) 125. Peya, Alexander *(128)* ....(AUT)
126. Salzenstein, Jeff *(109)*....................(USA)
(Q) 127. Wang, Yeu-Tzuoo *(181)* ....(TPE)
128. **Roddick, Andy [2] *(2)*** ....(USA)

Second Round

R.Federer [1] *(1)* 6/3 6/3 6/0
A.Falla *(138)* 2/6 6/3 6/1 6/3
F.Santoro *(53)* 7/5 6/2 3/6 6/2
T.Johansson *(23pr)* . 4/6 4/6 6/4 6/3 6/0
F.Lopez [18] *(22)* 6/4 6/2 7/5
C.Saulnier *(83)* . . . 7/5 4/6 7/6(6) 7/6(3)
G.Elseneer *(99)* . . . . 7/6(5) 7/6(5) 7/6(3)
I.Karlovic *(62)* 3/6 6/4 6/4 6/4
C.Moya [9] *(7)*. . . 6/4 3/6 7/5 6/7(6) 6/1
R.Stepanek *(67)* . . . 4/6 6/3 6/2 5/7 6/4
S.Sargsian *(48)* 6/4 6/3 4/6 6/2
D.Tursunov *(70)* . . . . 4/6 7/5 6/3 7/6(1)
G.Ivanisevic *(17pr)* . . . . . 6/3 7/6(4) 6/2
F.Volandri *(52)*........... 6/1 6/3 6/3
I.Labadze *(45)*........ 6/2 6/4 3/6 6/2
L.Hewitt [7] *(10)* 6/2 6/4 6/2
G.Coria [3] *(3)* 6/4 6/7(3) 6/3 6/7(3) 6/3
F.Mayer *(66)* ...... 7/6(4) 7/6(5) 7/6(4)
K.Kucera *(76)* 6/1 6/2 6/2
W.Ferreira *(82)* ..... 5/7 7/6(5) 7/5 6/2
J.Bjorkman [17] *(27)* . . . 5/7 6/1 7/5 6/1
Y.Lu *(101)* 6/3 4/6 6/3 6/2
J.Johansson *(43)*...... 6/2 7/6(3) 7/6(7)
M.Fish [14] *(20)*.......... 6/3 6/2 6/3
S.Grosjean [10] *(13)* 6/4 6/2 6/4
G.Carraz *(69)* .... 7/6(5) 6/4 6/4
D.Bracciali *(218)* . . 3/6 4/6 6/2 6/3 6/3
J-M.Gambill *(84)*......... 6/3 7/5 6/4
R.Ginepri [27] *(34)* 4/6 7/5 6/3 6/3
F.Verdasco *(40)* 6/4 6/4 6/4
S.Koubek *(95)* 4/6 6/4 6/1 6/1
J.C.Ferrero [6] *(5)* ...... 6/4 7/6(4) 6/3
T.Henman [5] *(6)*. . . . 4/6 7/6(6) 6/4 6/2
I.Heuberger *(137)* . . . 5/7 6/0 6/1 7/6(9)
D.Ferrer *(49)* . . . . . 7/6(5) 6/4 6/7(4) 7/5
H.Arazi [32] *(39)*......... 6/1 6/4 6/2
F.Gonzalez [24] *(26)* 6/4 6/2 6/4
I.Andreev *(64)*........ 2/6 6/2 6/0 6/3
M.Verkerk *(56)* 4/6 6/3 6/4 7/5
M.Philippoussis [11] *(17)* . . 6/3 6/4 6/2
X.Malisse *(51)* 6/3 6/4 6/4
T.Haas *(11pr)* . . . 2/6 2/6 7/6(8) 6/4 8/6
K.Beck *(71)*. . . . 6/4 6/7(3) 4/6 6/3 10/8
T.Robredo [20] *(19)*....... 6/4 6/4 6/4
D.Hrbaty [25] *(25)* 6/2 6/4 6/2
M.A.Hilton *(479)*......... 6/1 6/4 6/3
J.Benneteau *(80)* 6/3 7/5 6/4
M.Ancic *(63)*....... 6/7(5) 6/4 6/3 6/4
R.Schuettler [8] *(8)* . . 4/6 6/3 7/6(5) 1/6 6/2
G.Rusedski *(165)* 7/5 4/6 6/2 6/2
F.Mantilla *(127)*..... 7/6(5) 4/6 7/5 6/1
V.Spadea [30] *(30)*........ 6/2 6/4 6/2
J.I.Chela [21] *(18)* 6/4 4/6 6/0 6/2
T.Enqvist *(57)* .... 4/6 7/6(2) 6/4 7/6(1)
T.Martin *(72)*. . . . 4/6 6/3 7/6(1) 4/6 9/7
S.Schalken [12] *(23)* 6/2 6/1 6/3
A.Popp *(90)*............. 6/2 6/4 6/4
A.Montanes *(78)* 6/4 6/2 6/3
K.Carlsen *(103)* 3/6 7/6(5) 7/6(4) 6/7(0) 6/4
A.Pavel [22] *(21)* .... 6/3 7/5 7/6(8)
T.Dent [26] *(31)*.......... 6/2 6/3 6/4
S.Pescosolido *(143)* 4/6 4/6 6/4 7/6(5) 10/8
A.Peya *(128)* 6/2 6/4 6/2
A.Roddick [2] *(2)*......... 6/3 7/5 6/4

Third Round

R.Federer [1] *(1)* 6/1 6/2 6/0
T.Johansson *(23pr)* 7/5 6/2 6/1
F.Lopez [18] *(22)* .... 3/6 6/3 6/4 6/7(3) 8/6
I.Karlovic *(62)* .... 6/4 6/4 3/6 7/6(14)
C.Moya [9] *(7)* .... 6/4 6/4 6/7(5) 7/5
D.Tursunov *(70)* ...... 6/3 7/6(5) 3/6 4/6 15/13
G.Ivanisevic *(17pr)* .... 4/6 7/6(8) 1/6 6/3 6/4
L.Hewitt [7] *(10)* 6/4 6/4 6/1
F.Mayer *(66)* 4/6 6/3 6/3 6/4
W.Ferreira *(82)* .... 7/6(3) 6/3 6/1
J.Bjorkman [17] *(27)* 6/4 6/3 6/4
J.Johansson *(43)* .... 6/7(8) 6/3 6/4 6/4
S.Grosjean [10] *(13)* 6/1 6/2 6/2
J-M.Gambill *(84)* .... 6/7(4) 7/6(6) 6/3 6/2
R.Ginepri [27] *(34)* .... 6/7(3) 6/4 6/4 6/3
J.C.Ferrero [6] *(5)* .... 4/6 7/5 5/7 7/6(6) 8/6
T.Henman [5] *(6)* 7/5 6/3 6/2
H.Arazi [32] *(39)* .... 6/7(5) 6/4 6/3 7/6(7)
F.Gonzalez [24] *(26)* .... 7/5 6/3 5/7 6/7(4) 6/3
M.Philippoussis [11] *(17)* .... 4/6 6/3 7/6(5) 7/5
X.Malisse *(51)* 3/6 6/3 6/2 6/4
K.Beck *(71)* .... 6/3 6/2 7/6(2)
D.Hrbaty [25] *(25)* 7/5 6/4 6/2
M.Ancic *(63)* .... 4/6 7/6(8) 6/2 5/7 6/4
R.Schuettler [8] *(8)* . . . 6/7(5) 7/6(10) 6/7(5) 6/2 6/2
V.Spadea [30] *(30)* 6/1 6/2 6/2
T.Enqvist *(57)* .... 6/3 6/7(4) 6/1 3/6 6/3
S.Schalken [12] *(23)* 6/3 6/2 4/6 6/3
A.Popp *(90)* 6/1 6/0 6/1
K.Carlsen *(103)* .... 7/6(9) 6/4 6/3
T.Dent [26] *(31)* .... 6/3 6/3 7/6(3)
A.Roddick [2] *(2)* .... 6/3 7/6(2) 6/4

Fourth Round

R.Federer [1] *(1)* 6/3 6/4 6/3
I.Karlovic *(62)* ....7/6(12) 7/6(3) 6/7(2) 7/5
C.Moya [9] *(7)* 6/1 6/4 7/5
L.Hewitt [7] *(10)* 6/2 6/3 6/4
F.Mayer *(66)* 4/6 6/4 6/1 6/4
J.Johansson *(43)* ....6/7(5) 7/6(5) 7/6(6) 6/3
S.Grosjean [10] *(13)* ....7/6(5) 6/3 6/2
R.Ginepri [27] *(34)* 6/3 6/4 6/1
T.Henman [5] *(6)* ....7/6(6) 6/4 3/6 6/2
M.Philippoussis [11] *(17)* ....6/4 6/1 6/7(4) 7/5
X.Malisse *(51)* 6/3 6/3 6/4
M.Ancic *(63)* 7/5 6/3 7/5
V.Spadea [30] *(30)* 6/4 6/2 6/3
S.Schalken [12] *(23)* ....5/7 6/2 3/6 7/6(8) 6/2
A.Popp *(90)* 7/5 6/4 6/4
A.Roddick [2] *(2)* ....6/3 7/6(6) 7/6(1)

Quarter-Finals

R.Federer [1] *(1)* ....6/3 7/6(3) 7/6(5)
L.Hewitt [7] *(10)* ....6/4 6/2 4/6 7/6(3)
F.Mayer *(66)* ....6/3 6/7(5) 7/6(5) 6/4
S.Grosjean [10] *(13)* ....6/2 6/2 7/6(4)
T.Henman [5] *(6)* ....6/2 7/5 6/7(3) 7/6(5)
M.Ancic *(63)* ....7/5 3/1 Ret'd.
S.Schalken [12] *(23)* 6/2 7/5 3/6 6/2
A.Roddick [2] *(2)* 7/5 6/4 6/4

Semi-Finals

R.Federer [1] *(1)* 6/1 6/7(1) 6/0 6/4
S.Grosjean [10] *(13)* 7/5 6/4 6/2
M.Ancic *(63)* 7/6(5) 6/4 6/2
A.Roddick [2] *(2)* 7/6(4) 7/6(9) 6/3

Final

R.Federer [1] *(1)* 6/2 6/3 7/6(6)
A.Roddick [2] *(2)* 6/4 4/6 7/5 7/5

R.Federer [1] *(1)* 4/6 7/5 7/6(3) 6/4

Heavy type denotes seeded players. The figure in brackets against names denotes the order in which they have been seeded. (W) = Wild card. (Q) = Qualifier. (L) = Lucky loser.

The matches are the best of five sets

The winners become the holders, for the year only, of the CHALLENGE CUPS presented by the OXFORD UNIVERSITY LAWN TENNIS CLUB and the late SIR HERBERT WILBERFORCE respectively. The winners receive silver replicas of the two Challenge Cups. A silver salver is presented to each of the runners-up, and a bronze medal to each defeated semi-finalist.

First Round	Second Round	Third Round	Quarter-Finals	Semi-Finals	Final

1. **J.Bjorkman** (SWE) **& T.A.Woodbridge** (AUS) ....[1]
2. A.Martin (ESP) & A.Montanes (ESP)

   J.Bjorkman & T.A.Woodbridge [1]
   ....6/1 6/2

3. L.Arnold (ARG) & M.Garcia (ARG)
4. J.Coetzee (RSA) & C.Haggard (RSA)

   L.Arnold & M.Garcia
   ....7/6(3) 7/6(4)

J.Bjorkman & T.A.Woodbridge [1]
.....................................6/3 6/2

5. R.Leach (USA) & B.MacPhie (USA)
(Q) 6. R.De Voest (RSA) & N.Healey (AUS)

   R.Leach & B.MacPhie
   ....7/6(4) 6/4

7. T.Cibulec (CZE) & P.Pala (CZE)
8. **X.Malisse** (BEL) **& O.Rochus** (BEL) ....[14]

   X.Malisse & O.Rochus [14]
   ....6/1 7/6(2)

R.Leach & B.MacPhie
.... 6/7(3) 7/5 4/5 retired

J.Bjorkman & T.A.Woodbridge [1]
...................................3/6 6/4 9/7

9. **G.Etlis** (ARG) **& M.Rodriguez** (ARG) ....[9]
(W) 10. J.Auckland (GBR) & L.Childs (GBR)

   G.Etlis & M.Rodriguez [9]
   ....6/4 6/3

11. D.Ferrer (ESP) & R.Ramirez Hidalgo (ESP)
12. N.Davydenko (RUS) & A.Fisher (AUS)

   N.Davydenko & A.Fisher
   ....6/2 6/1

N.Davydenko & A.Fisher
.... 7/5 7/6(2)

13. D.Bowen (USA) & T.Phillips (USA)
(W) 14. I.Flanagan (GBR) & M.Lee (GBR)

   I.Flanagan & M.Lee
   ....3/6 7/6(5) 7/5

15. K.Braasch (GER) & R.Schuettler (GER)
16. **M.Damm** (CZE) **& C.Suk** (CZE) ....[8]

   M.Damm & C.Suk [8]
   ....6/0 6/4

M.Damm & C.Suk [8]
.... 7/6(4) 7/6(5)

N.Davydenko & A.Fisher
................6/7(4) 7/6(6) 15/13

J.Bjorkman & T.A.Woodbridge [1]
7/5 6/2

(L) 17. D.Ayala (USA) & B.Vahaly (USA)
18. A.Lopez Moron (ESP) & D.Skoch (CZE)

   A.Lopez Moron & D.Skoch
   ....1/6 6/1 7/5

19. J.Levinsky (CZE) & F.Volandri (ITA)
20. S.Aspelin (SWE) & T.Perry (AUS)

   S.Aspelin & T.Perry
   ....6/2 6/2

S.Aspelin & T.Perry
.... 6/3 6/7(5) 8/6

21. F.Mayer (GER) & R.Wassen (NED)
22. J-F.Bachelot (FRA) & A.Pavel (ROM)

   J-F.Bachelot & A.Pavel
   ....6/3 6/4

23. J.Kerr (AUS) & T.Vanhoudt (BEL)
24. **M.Hood** (ARG) **& S.Prieto** (ARG) ....[15]

   M.Hood & S.Prieto [15]
   ....7/6(4) 6/2

J-F.Bachelot & A.Pavel
.... 6/2 7/6(7)

S.Aspelin & T.Perry
................6/4 6/2

25. **J.Erlich** (ISR) **& A.Ram** (ISR) ....[10]
26. J.Novak (CZE) & R.Stepanek (CZE)

   J.Novak & R.Stepanek
   ....6/4 7/6(4)

27. S.Sargsian (ARM) & M.Youzhny (RUS)
(Q) 28. S.Huss (AUS) & R.Lindstedt (SWE)

   S.Huss & R.Lindstedt
   ....6/3 6/4

J.Novak & R.Stepanek
.... 6/4 3/6 6/3

(L) 29. K.Carlsen (DEN) & T.Ketola (FIN)
30. F.Lopez (ESP) & F.Verdasco (ESP)

   F.Lopez & F.Verdasco
   ....6/3 6/4

(W) 31. A.Banks (GBR) & A.Bogdanovic (GBR)
32. **W.Arthurs** (AUS) **& P.Hanley** (AUS) ....[7]

   W.Arthurs & P.Hanley [7]
   ....7/6(4) 6/2

W.Arthurs & P.Hanley [7]
.... 7/6(2) 6/4

W.Arthurs & P.Hanley [7]
................7/6(4) 6/4

W.Arthurs & P.Hanley [7]
6/3 7/6(3)

33. **W.Black** (ZIM) **& K.Ullyett** (ZIM) ....[6]
34. F.Browne (ARG) & G.Coria (ARG)

   W.Black & K.Ullyett [6]
   ....6/3 6/2

35. A.Sa (BRA) & F.Saretta (BRA)
36. I.Karlovic (CRO) & J.Thomas (USA)

   A.Sa & F.Saretta
   ....3/6 7/6(2) 12/10

W.Black & K.Ullyett [6]
.... 4/6 6/3 6/4

37. J.Benneteau (FRA) & N.Mahut (FRA)
38. F.Mantilla (ESP) & N.Massu (CHI)

   J.Benneteau & N.Mahut
   ....4/6 7/6(4) 17/15

39. J-M.Gambill (USA) & M.Hill (AUS)
40. **J.Palmer** (USA) **& P.Vizner** (CZE) ....[12]

   J.Palmer & P.Vizner [12]
   ....6/2 6/4

J.Palmer & P.Vizner [12]
.... 6/4 6/3

W.Black & K.Ullyett [6]
................7/5 6/4

41. **J.Knowle** (AUT) **& N.Zimonjic** (SCG) ....[16]
42. Y.Allegro (SUI) & M.Kohlmann (GER)

   J.Knowle & N.Zimonjic [16]
   ....6/4 6/4

43. M.Fyrstenberg (POL) & M.Matkowski (POL)
44. I.Andreev (RUS) & D.Sanchez (ESP)

   M.Fyrstenberg & M.Matkowski
   ....6/1 6/2

J.Knowle & N.Zimonjic [16]
.... 7/6(6) 7/6(3)

45. R.Sluiter (NED) & M.Verkerk (NED)
46. J.Carrasco (ESP) & T.Robredo (ESP)

   R.Sluiter & M.Verkerk
   ....6/3 6/7(8) 6/3

47. H.Arazi (MAR) & J.Eagle (AUS)
48. **M.Bhupathi** (IND) **& M.Mirnyi** (BLR) ....[3]

   M.Bhupathi & M.Mirnyi [3]
   ....6/3 6/4

M.Bhupathi & M.Mirnyi [3]
.... 7/5 6/3

J.Knowle & N.Zimonjic [16]
................6/4 3/6 8/6

J.Knowle & N.Zimonjic [16]
7/5 4/6 6/4

49. **M.Knowles** (BAH) **& D.Nestor** (CAN) ....[5]
50. R.Ginepri (USA) & M.Merklein (BAH)

   M.Knowles & D.Nestor [5]
   ....6/1 6/3

51. M.Bertolini (ITA) & R.Koenig (RSA)
52. T.Johansson (SWE) & J.Landsberg (SWE)

   T.Johansson & J.Landsberg
   ....6/3 6/4

M.Knowles & D.Nestor [5]
.... 6/2 6/4

53. T.Parrott (USA) & V.Spadea (USA)
(W) 54. M.A.Hilton (GBR) & J.Murray (GBR)

   T.Parrott & V.Spadea
   ....6/7(5) 7/6(4) 6/4

55. D.Bracciali (ITA) & G.Galimberti (ITA) (Q)
56. **L.Paes** (IND) **& D.Rikl** (CZE) ....[11]

   L.Paes & D.Rikl [11]
   ....7/5 6/7(3) 6/3

T.Parrott & V.Spadea
.... 7/6(6) 6/3

M.Knowles & D.Nestor [5]
................6/3 6/2

57. **F.Cermak** (CZE) **& L.Friedl** (CZE) ....[13]
58. J.Gimelstob (USA) & S.Humphries (USA)

   J.Gimelstob & S.Humphries
   ....7/6(3) 6/4

(W) 59. D.Kiernan (GBR) & D.Sherwood (GBR)
60. D.Hrbaty (SVK) & G.Oliver (USA)

   D.Hrbaty & G.Oliver
   ....7/6(6) 6/4

J.Gimelstob & S.Humphries
.... 6/3 6/7(1) 6/3

61. J.I.Chela (ARG) & L.Horna (PER)
(Q) 62. G.Kisgyorgy (HUN) & L.Kubot (POL)

   G.Kisgyorgy & L.Kubot
   ....6/3 3/6 9/7

(W) 63. J.Delgado (GBR) & A.Parmar (GBR)
64. **B.Bryan** (USA) **& M.Bryan** (USA) ....[2]

   B.Bryan & M.Bryan [2]
   ....6/4 6/3

B.Bryan & M.Bryan [2]
.... 7/6(6) 6/3

J.Gimelstob & S.Humphries
................6/3 3/6 6/4

M.Knowles & D.Nestor [5]
6/3 6/2

J.Bjorkman & T.A.Woodbridge [1]
7/5 7/5 7/6(4)

J.Knowle & N.Zimonjic [16]
6/2 3/6 6/3 6/7(7) 6/3

J.Bjorkman & T.A.Woodbridge [1]
6/1 6/4 4/6 6/4

Heavy type denotes seeded players. The figure in brackets against names denotes the order in which they have been seeded. (W) = Wild card. (Q) = Qualifier. (L) = Lucky loser.
The matches are the best of three sets up to the third round, best of five sets thereafter

THE LADIES' SINGLES CHAMPIONSHIP

Holder: Miss S Williams

The winner becomes the holder, for the year only, of the CHALLENGE TROPHY presented by The All England Lawn Tennis and Croquet Club. The winner receives a silver replica of the Trophy. A silver salver is presented to the runner-up and a bronze medal to each defeated semi-finalist.

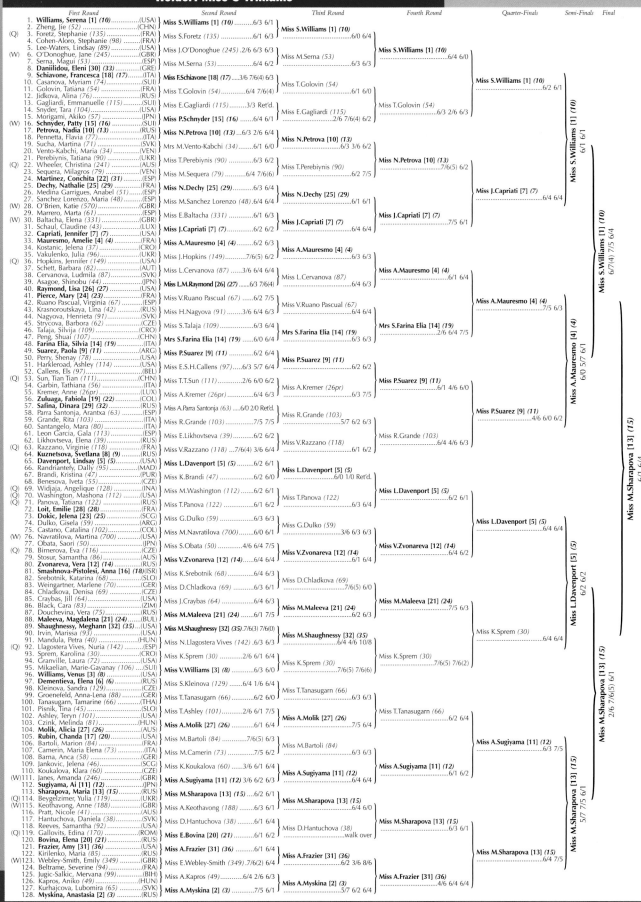

First Round

1. **Williams, Serena [1] *(10)*** ....(USA)
2. Zheng, Jie *(52)* ....(CHN)
3. (Q) Foretz, Stephanie *(135)* ....(FRA)
4. Cohen-Aloro, Stephanie *(98)* ....(FRA)
5. Lee-Waters, Lindsay *(89)* ....(USA)
6. (W) O'Donoghue, Jane *(245)* ....(GBR)
7. Serna, Magui *(53)* ....(ESP)
8. **Daniilidou, Eleni [30] *(33)*** ....(GRE)
9. **Schiavone, Francesca [18] *(17)*** ....(ITA)
10. Casanova, Myriam *(74)* ....(SUI)
11. Golovin, Tatiana *(54)* ....(FRA)
12. Jidkova, Alina *(76)* ....(RUS)
13. Gagliardi, Emmanuelle *(115)* ....(SUI)
14. Snyder, Tara *(104)* ....(USA)
15. Morigami, Akiko *(57)* ....(JPN)
16. (W) **Schnyder, Patty [15] *(16)*** ....(SUI)
17. **Petrova, Nadia [10] *(13)*** ....(RUS)
18. Pennetta, Flavia *(77)* ....(ITA)
19. Sucha, Martina *(71)* ....(SVK)
20. Vento-Kabchi, Maria *(34)* ....(VEN)
21. Perebiynis, Tatiana *(90)* ....(UKR)
22. (Q) Wheeler, Christina *(241)* ....(AUS)
23. Sequera, Milagros *(79)* ....(VEN)
24. **Martinez, Conchita [22] *(31)*** ....(ESP)
25. **Dechy, Nathalie [25] *(29)*** ....(FRA)
26. Medina Garrigues, Anabel *(51)* ....(ESP)
27. Sanchez Lorenzo, Maria *(48)* ....(ESP)
28. (W) O'Brien, Katie *(570)* ....(GBR)
29. Marrero, Marta *(61)* ....(ESP)
30. (W) Baltacha, Elena *(331)* ....(GBR)
31. Schaul, Claudine *(43)* ....(LUX)
32. **Capriati, Jennifer [7] *(7)*** ....(USA)
33. **Mauresmo, Amelie [4] *(4)*** ....(FRA)
34. Kostanic, Jelena *(37)* ....(CRO)
35. Vakulenko, Julia *(96)* ....(UKR)
36. (Q) Hopkins, Jennifer *(149)* ....(USA)
37. Schett, Barbara *(82)* ....(AUT)
38. Cervanova, Ludmila *(87)* ....(SVK)
39. Asagoe, Shinobu *(44)* ....(JPN)
40. **Raymond, Lisa [26] *(27)*** ....(USA)
41. **Pierce, Mary [24] *(23)*** ....(FRA)
42. Ruano Pascual, Virginia *(67)* ....(ESP)
43. Krasnoroutskaya, Lina *(42)* ....(RUS)
44. Nagyova, Henrieta *(91)* ....(SVK)
45. Strycova, Barbora *(62)* ....(CZE)
46. Talaja, Silvija *(109)* ....(CRO)
47. Peng, Shuai *(107)* ....(CHN)
48. **Farina Elia, Silvia [14] *(19)*** ....(ITA)
49. **Suarez, Paola [9] *(11)*** ....(ARG)
50. Perry, Shenay *(78)* ....(USA)
51. Harkleroad, Ashley *(114)* ....(USA)
52. Callens, Els *(97)* ....(BEL)
53. (Q) Sun, Tian Tian *(111)* ....(CHN)
54. Garbin, Tathiana *(56)* ....(ITA)
55. Kremer, Anne *(26pr)* ....(LUX)
56. **Zuluaga, Fabiola [19] *(22)*** ....(COL)
57. **Safina, Dinara [29] *(32)*** ....(RUS)
58. Parra Santonja, Arantxa *(63)* ....(ESP)
59. Grande, Rita *(103)* ....(ITA)
60. Santangelo, Mara *(80)* ....(ITA)
61. Leon Garcia, Gala *(113)* ....(ESP)
62. Likhovtseva, Elena *(39)* ....(RUS)
63. (Q) Razzano, Virginie *(118)* ....(FRA)
64. **Kuznetsova, Svetlana [8] *(9)*** ....(RUS)
65. **Davenport, Lindsay [5] *(5)*** ....(USA)
66. Randriantefy, Dally *(95)* ....(MAD)
67. Brandi, Kristina *(47)* ....(PUR)
68. Benesova, Iveta *(55)* ....(CZE)
69. (Q) Widjaja, Angelique *(128)* ....(INA)
70. (Q) Washington, Mashona *(112)* ....(USA)
71. (Q) Panova, Tatiana *(122)* ....(RUS)
72. **Loit, Emilie [28] *(28)*** ....(FRA)
73. **Dokic, Jelena [23] *(25)*** ....(SCG)
74. Dulko, Gisela *(59)* ....(ARG)
75. Castano, Catalina *(102)* ....(COL)
76. (W) Navratilova, Martina *(700)* ....(USA)
77. Obata, Saori *(50)* ....(JPN)
78. (Q) Birnerova, Eva *(116)* ....(CZE)
79. Stosur, Samantha *(86)* ....(AUS)
80. **Zvonareva, Vera [12] *(14)*** ....(RUS)
81. **Smashnova-Pistolesi, Anna [16] *(18)*** (ISR)
82. Srebotnik, Katarina *(68)* ....(SLO)
83. Weingartner, Marlene *(70)* ....(GER)
84. Chladkova, Denisa *(69)* ....(CZE)
85. Craybas, Jill *(64)* ....(USA)
86. Black, Cara *(83)* ....(ZIM)
87. Douchevina, Vera *(75)* ....(RUS)
88. **Maleeva, Magdalena [21] *(24)*** ....(BUL)
89. **Shaughnessy, Meghann [32] *(35)*** ....(USA)
90. Irvin, Marissa *(93)* ....(USA)
91. Mandula, Petra *(40)* ....(HUN)
92. (Q) Llagostera Vives, Nuria *(142)* ....(ESP)
93. Sprem, Karolina *(30)* ....(CRO)
94. Granville, Laura *(72)* ....(USA)
95. Mikaelian, Marie-Gayanay *(106)* ....(SUI)
96. **Williams, Venus [3] *(8)*** ....(USA)
97. **Dementieva, Elena [6] *(6)*** ....(RUS)
98. Kleinova, Sandra *(129)* ....(CZE)
99. Groenefeld, Anna-Lena *(88)* ....(GER)
100. Tanasugarn, Tamarine *(66)* ....(THA)
101. Pisnik, Tina *(45)* ....(SLO)
102. Ashley, Teryn *(101)* ....(USA)
103. Czink, Melinda *(81)* ....(HUN)
104. **Molik, Alicia [27] *(26)*** ....(AUS)
105. **Rubin, Chanda [17] *(20)*** ....(USA)
106. Bartoli, Marion *(84)* ....(FRA)
107. Camerin, Maria Elena *(73)* ....(ITA)
108. Barna, Anca *(58)* ....(GER)
109. Jankovic, Jelena *(46)* ....(SCG)
110. Koukalova, Klara *(60)* ....(CZE)
111. (W) Janes, Amanda *(246)* ....(GBR)
112. **Sugiyama, Ai [11] *(12)*** ....(JPN)
113. **Sharapova, Maria [13] *(15)*** ....(RUS)
114. (Q) Beygelzimer, Yulia *(119)* ....(UKR)
115. (W) Keothavong, Anne *(188)* ....(GBR)
116. Pratt, Nicole *(41)* ....(AUS)
117. Hantuchova, Daniela *(38)* ....(SVK)
118. Reeves, Samantha *(92)* ....(USA)
119. (Q) Gallovits, Edina *(170)* ....(ROM)
120. **Bovina, Elena [20] *(21)*** ....(RUS)
121. **Frazier, Amy [31] *(36)*** ....(USA)
122. Kirilenko, Maria *(85)* ....(RUS)
123. (W) Webley-Smith, Emily *(349)* ....(GBR)
124. Beltrame, Severine *(94)* ....(FRA)
125. Jugic-Salkic, Mervana *(99)* ....(BIH)
126. Kapros, Aniko *(49)* ....(HUN)
127. Kurhajcova, Lubomira *(65)* ....(SVK)
128. **Myskina, Anastasia [2] *(3)*** ....(RUS)

Second Round

- **Miss S.Williams [1] *(10)*** 6/3 6/1
- Miss S.Foretz *(135)* 6/1 6/3
- Miss J.O'Donoghue *(245)* .2/6 6/3 6/3
- Miss M.Serna *(53)* 6/4 6/2
- **Miss F.Schiavone [18] *(17)*** .....3/6 7/6(4) 6/3
- Miss T.Golovin *(54)* ....6/4 7/6(4)
- Miss E.Gagliardi *(115)* ....3/3 Ret'd.
- **Miss P.Schnyder [15] *(16)*** 6/4 6/1
- **Miss N.Petrova [10] *(13)*** ...6/3 2/6 6/4
- Mrs M.Vento-Kabchi *(34)* 6/1 6/0
- Miss T.Perebiynis *(90)* 6/3 6/2
- Miss M.Sequera *(79)* ....6/4 7/6(6)
- **Miss N.Dechy [25] *(29)*** 6/3 6/4
- Miss M.Sanchez Lorenzo *(48)* .6/4 6/4
- Miss E.Baltacha *(331)* 6/1 6/3
- **Miss J.Capriati [7] *(7)*** 6/2 6/2
- **Miss A.Mauresmo [4] *(4)*** 6/2 6/3
- Miss J.Hopkins *(149)* ....7/6(5) 6/2
- Miss L.Cervanova *(87)* 3/6 6/4 6/4
- **Miss L.M.Raymond [26] *(27)*** ....6/3 7/6(4)
- Miss V.Ruano Pascual *(67)* 6/2 7/5
- Miss H.Nagyova *(91)* 3/6 6/4 6/3
- Miss S.Talaja *(109)* 6/3 6/4
- **Mrs S.Farina Elia [14] *(19)*** 6/0 6/4
- **Miss P.Suarez [9] *(11)*** 6/2 6/4
- Miss E.S.H.Callens *(97)* 6/3 5/7 6/4
- Miss T.T.Sun *(111)* 2/6 6/0 6/2
- Miss A.Kremer *(26pr)* 6/4 6/3
- Miss A.Parra Santonja *(63)* .....6/0 2/0 Ret'd.
- Miss R.Grande *(103)* 7/5 7/5
- Miss E.Likhovtseva *(39)* 6/2 6/2
- Miss V.Razzano *(118)* ...7/6(4) 3/6 6/4
- **Miss L.Davenport [5] *(5)*** 6/2 6/1
- Miss K.Brandi *(47)* 6/2 6/0
- Miss M.Washington *(112)* 6/2 6/1
- Miss T.Panova *(122)* 6/1 6/2
- Miss G.Dulko *(59)* 6/3 6/3
- Miss M.Navratilova *(700)* 6/0 6/1
- Miss S.Obata *(50)* 4/6 6/4 7/5
- **Miss V.Zvonareva [12] *(14)*** 6/4 6/4
- Miss K.Srebotnik *(68)* 6/4 6/3
- Miss D.Chladkova *(69)* 6/3 6/1
- Miss J.Craybas *(64)* 6/4 6/3
- **Miss M.Maleeva [21] *(24)*** 6/1 7/5
- **Miss M.Shaughnessy [32] *(35)*** .7/6(3) 7/6(0)
- Miss N.Llagostera Vives *(142)* .6/3 6/3
- Miss K.Sprem *(30)* 2/6 6/1 6/4
- **Miss V.Williams [3] *(8)*** 6/3 6/0
- Miss S.Kleinova *(129)* 6/4 1/6 6/4
- Miss T.Tanasugarn *(66)* 6/2 6/0
- Miss T.Ashley *(101)* 2/6 6/1 7/5
- **Miss A.Molik [27] *(26)*** 6/1 6/4
- Miss M.Bartoli *(84)* ....7/6(5) 6/3
- Miss M.Camerin *(73)* 7/5 6/2
- Miss K.Koukalova *(60)* 3/6 6/1 6/4
- **Miss A.Sugiyama [11] *(12)*** 3/6 6/2 6/3
- **Miss M.Sharapova [13] *(15)*** 6/2 6/1
- Miss A.Keothavong *(188)* 6/3 6/1
- Miss D.Hantuchova *(38)* 6/1 6/4
- **Miss E.Bovina [20] *(21)*** 6/1 6/2
- **Miss A.Frazier [31] *(36)*** 6/1 6/4
- Miss E.Webley-Smith *(349)* .7/6(2) 6/4
- Miss A.Kapros *(49)* 6/4 2/6 6/3
- **Miss A.Myskina [2] *(3)*** 7/5 6/1

Third Round

- **Miss S.Williams [1] *(10)*** 6/0 6/4
- Miss M.Serna *(53)* 6/3 6/3
- Miss T.Golovin *(54)* 6/1 6/0
- Miss E.Gagliardi *(115)* ....2/6 7/6(4) 6/2
- **Miss N.Petrova [10] *(13)*** 6/3 3/6 6/2
- Miss T.Perebiynis *(90)* 6/2 7/5
- **Miss N.Dechy [25] *(29)*** 6/1 6/1
- **Miss J.Capriati [7] *(7)*** 6/4 6/4
- **Miss A.Mauresmo [4] *(4)*** 6/3 6/3
- Miss L.Cervanova *(87)* 6/4 6/3
- Miss V.Ruano Pascual *(67)* 6/4 6/4
- **Mrs S.Farina Elia [14] *(19)*** 6/3 6/3
- **Miss P.Suarez [9] *(11)*** 6/2 6/2
- Miss A.Kremer *(26pr)* 6/3 7/5
- Miss R.Grande *(103)* 5/7 6/2 6/3
- Miss V.Razzano *(118)* 6/1 6/2
- **Miss L.Davenport [5] *(5)*** ....6/0 1/0 Ret'd.
- Miss T.Panova *(122)* 6/3 6/4
- Miss G.Dulko *(59)* 3/6 6/3 6/3
- **Miss V.Zvonareva [12] *(14)*** 6/1 6/4
- Miss D.Chladkova *(69)* ....7/6(5) 6/0
- **Miss M.Maleeva [21] *(24)*** 6/2 6/3
- **Miss M.Shaughnessy [32] *(35)*** 6/4 4/6 10/8
- Miss K.Sprem *(30)* ....7/6(5) 7/6(6)
- Miss T.Tanasugarn *(66)* 6/3 6/3
- **Miss A.Molik [27] *(26)*** 7/5 6/4
- Miss M.Bartoli *(84)* 6/3 6/3
- **Miss A.Sugiyama [11] *(12)*** 6/4 6/4
- **Miss M.Sharapova [13] *(15)*** 6/4 6/0
- Miss D.Hantuchova *(38)* ....walk over
- **Miss A.Frazier [31] *(36)*** 6/2 3/6 8/6
- **Miss A.Myskina [2] *(3)*** 5/7 6/2 6/4

Fourth Round

- **Miss S.Williams [1] *(10)*** 6/4 6/0
- Miss T.Golovin *(54)* 6/3 2/6 6/3
- **Miss N.Petrova [10] *(13)*** ....7/6(5) 6/2
- **Miss J.Capriati [7] *(7)*** 7/5 6/1
- **Miss A.Mauresmo [4] *(4)*** 6/1 6/4
- **Mrs S.Farina Elia [14] *(19)*** 2/6 6/4 7/5
- **Miss P.Suarez [9] *(11)*** 6/1 4/6 6/0
- Miss R.Grande *(103)* 6/4 4/6 6/3
- **Miss L.Davenport [5] *(5)*** 6/2 6/1
- **Miss V.Zvonareva [12] *(14)*** 6/4 6/2
- **Miss M.Maleeva [21] *(24)*** 7/5 6/3
- Miss K.Sprem *(30)* ....7/6(5) 7/6(2)
- Miss T.Tanasugarn *(66)* 6/2 6/4
- **Miss A.Sugiyama [11] *(12)*** 6/1 6/2
- **Miss M.Sharapova [13] *(15)*** 6/3 6/1
- **Miss A.Frazier [31] *(36)*** 4/6 6/4 6/4

Quarter-Finals

- **Miss S.Williams [1] *(10)*** 6/2 6/1
- **Miss J.Capriati [7] *(7)*** 6/4 6/4
- **Miss A.Mauresmo [4] *(4)*** 7/5 6/3
- **Miss P.Suarez [9] *(11)*** 4/6 6/0 6/2
- **Miss L.Davenport [5] *(5)*** 6/4 6/4
- Miss K.Sprem *(30)* 6/4 6/4
- **Miss A.Sugiyama [11] *(12)*** 6/3 7/5
- **Miss M.Sharapova [13] *(15)*** 6/4 7/5

Semi-Finals

- **Miss S.Williams [1] *(10)*** 6/1 6/1
- **Miss A.Mauresmo [4] *(4)*** 6/0 5/7 6/1
- **Miss L.Davenport [5] *(5)*** 6/2 6/2
- **Miss M.Sharapova [13] *(15)*** 5/7 7/5 6/1

Final

- **Miss S.Williams [1] *(10)*** 6/7(4) 7/5 6/4
- **Miss M.Sharapova [13] *(15)*** 2/6 7/6(5) 6/1

Miss M.Sharapova [13] *(15)* 6/1 6/4

Heavy type denotes seeded players. The figure in brackets against names denotes the order in which they have been seeded. (W) = Wild card. (Q) = Qualifier. (L) = Lucky loser.

The matches are the best of three sets

The winners become the holders, for the year only, of the CHALLENGE CUP presented by HRH PRINCESS MARINA, DUCHESS OF KENT, the late President of The All England Lawn Tennis and Croquet Club. The winners receive silver replicas of the Challenge Cup. A silver salver is presented to each of the runners-up and a bronze medal to each defeated semi-finalist.

First Round	Second Round	Third Round	Quarter-Finals	Semi-Finals	Final

1. Miss V.Ruano Pascual (ESP) & Miss P.Suarez (ARG) ....[1]
(L) 2. Miss A.Augustus (USA) & Miss N.Grandin (RSA) ......
    Miss V.Ruano Pascual & Miss P.Suarez [1] 6/2 6/2

3. Miss O.Blahotova (CZE) & Miss G.Navratilova (CZE) .....
4. Miss S.Asagoe (JPN) & Miss R.Fujiwara (JPN) ....
    Miss S.Asagoe & Miss R.Fujiwara 4/6 6/3 6/3

    Miss V.Ruano Pascual & Miss P.Suarez [1] ....7/6(2) 6/1

(Q) 5. Miss L.Bacheva (BUL) & Miss E.Birnerova (CZE) .....
6. Miss G.Dulko (ARG) & Miss P.Tarabini (ARG) ....
    Miss G.Dulko & Miss P.Tarabini 6/3 6/1

7. Miss I.Benesova (CZE) & Miss M.Pastikova (CZE) .....
8. Mrs S.Farina Elia (ITA) & Miss F.Schiavone (ITA) [14]
    Mrs S.Farina Elia & Miss F.Schiavone [14] 6/2 6/4

    Miss G.Dulko & Miss P.Tarabini

    Miss V.Ruano Pascual & Miss P.Suarez [1] 6/3 3/6 6/3

9. Miss A.Molik (AUS) & Miss M.Serna (ESP) ....[17]
(Q) 10. Miss L.Baker (NZL) & Miss N.Sewell (AUS) ....
    Miss A.Molik & Miss M.Serna [17] 6/3 7/5

(W) 11. Miss E.Baltacha (GBR) & Miss A.Janes (GBR) ....
(W) 12. Miss T.Golovin (FRA) & Miss M.Pierce (FRA) ....
    Miss T.Golovin & Miss M.Pierce 6/3 6/2

    Miss T.Golovin & Miss M.Pierce ....7/6(5) 6/7(5) 6/1

13. Miss W.Prakusya (INA) & Miss T.Tanasugarn (THA) ..
14. Miss L.McShea (AUS) & Miss M.Sequera (VEN) ......
    Miss W.Prakusya & Miss T.Tanasugarn 6/1 6/3

15. Mrs A.Svensson (SWE) & Miss M.Tu (USA) ....
16. Mrs M.Vento-Kabchi (VEN) & Miss A.Widjaja (INA) [8]
    Mrs M.Vento-Kabchi & Miss A.Widjaja [8] 6/4 6/2

    Mrs M.Vento-Kabchi & Miss A.Widjaja [8] 6/4 3/6 16/14

    Mrs M.Vento-Kabchi & Miss A.Widjaja [8] ....3/6 7/6(3) 6/1

    Miss V.Ruano Pascual & Miss P.Suarez [1] 5/7 6/4 6/3

17. Miss N.Petrova (RUS) & Miss M.Shaughnessy (USA) [4]
18. Miss C.Dhenin (FRA) & Miss E.Kulikovskaya (RUS) ..
    Miss N.Petrova & Miss M.Shaughnessy [4] 6/2 6/3

19. Miss N.Miyagi (JPN) & Miss M.Washington (USA) ....
20. Miss J.Kostanic (CRO) & Miss J.Lee (TPE) ....
    Miss J.Kostanic & Miss J.Lee 3/6 6/4 6/2

    Miss N.Petrova & Miss M.Shaughnessy [4] 6/2 6/2

21. Miss M.Ani (EST) & Miss S.Talaja (CRO) ....
22. Miss A.Cargill (USA) & Miss C.Wheeler (AUS) ....
    Miss A.Cargill & Miss C.Wheeler 6/4 3/6 6/4

23. Miss T.Ashley (USA) & Miss S.Perry (USA) ....
24. Miss E.S.H.Callens (BEL) & Miss P.Mandula (HUN) [15]
    Miss E.S.H.Callens & Miss P.Mandula [15] 6/4 6/4

    Miss E.S.H.Callens & Miss P.Mandula [15] 6/4 6/3

    Miss N.Petrova & Miss M.Shaughnessy [4] 6/3 6/0

25. Miss T.Li (CHN) & Miss T.T.Sun (CHN) ....[12]
(Q) 26. Miss E.Dominikovic (AUS) & Miss A.Rodionova (RUS)
    Miss E.Dominikovic & Miss A.Rodionova 6/2 6/3

27. Miss J.Jugic-Salkic (BIH) & Miss D.Jurak (CRO) ....
28. Miss B.Schett (AUT) & Miss P.Schnyder (SUI) ....
    Miss B.Schett & Miss P.Schnyder 6/2 4/6 6/2

    Miss B.Schett & Miss P.Schnyder 6/1 6/4

29. Miss L.Kurhajcova (SVK) & Miss L.Prusova (CZE) ....
30. Miss T.Garbin (ITA) & Miss T.Krizan (SLO) ....
    Miss T.Garbin & Miss T.Krizan 6/4 6/3

31. Miss J.Hopkins (USA) & Miss A.Spears (USA) ....
32. Miss C.Black (ZIM) & Miss R.P.Stubbs (AUS) ....[6]
    Miss C.Black & Miss R.P.Stubbs [6] 6/2 6/3

    Miss C.Black & Miss R.P.Stubbs [6] ....7/6(3) 6/3

    Miss C.Black & Miss R.P.Stubbs [6] ....7/6(5) 6/4

    Miss C.Black & Miss R.P.Stubbs [6] 6/4 6/3

33. Miss J.Husarova (SVK) & Miss C.Martinez (ESP) ..[7]
(W) 34. Miss A.Medina Garrigues (ESP) & Miss A.Sanchez Vicario (ESP)
    Miss J.Husarova & Miss C.Martinez [7] 6/2 6/2

35. Miss B.Rittner (GER) & Miss P.Wartusch (AUT) ....
36. Miss R.Grande (ITA) & Miss F.Pennetta (ITA) ....
    Miss R.Grande & Miss F.Pennetta 7/5 3/6 6/3

    Miss J.Husarova & Miss C.Martinez [7] 3/6 6/1 6/1

37. Miss K.Liggan (IRL) & Miss A.Parra Santonja (ESP) .
(L) 38. Miss B.Schwartz (AUT) & Miss J.Woehr (GER) ....
    Miss B.Schwartz & Miss J.Woehr 6/4 4/6 7/5

39. Miss M.Camerin (ITA) & Miss A.Jidkova (RUS) ....
40. Miss M.Bartoli (FRA) & Miss E.Loit (FRA) ....[11]
    Miss M.Bartoli & Miss E.Loit [11] 6/4 6/1

    Miss M.Bartoli & Miss E.Loit [11] 6/1 6/3

    Miss M.Bartoli & Miss E.Loit [11] 6/4 3/6 6/4

    Miss M.Navratilova & Miss L.M.Raymond [3] 6/2 6/4

41. Miss A.Myskina (RUS) & Miss V.Zvonareva (RUS) ..[13]
42. Miss S.Reeves (USA) & Miss E.Tatarkova (UKR) ......
    Miss A.Myskina & Miss V.Zvonareva [13] 6/4 6/2

43. Mrs J.Russell (USA) & Miss M.Santangelo (ITA) ....
44. Miss E.Daniilidou (GRE) & Miss K.Srebotnik (SLO) ..
    Mrs J.Russell & Miss M.Santangelo 6/2 5/7 6/4

    Mrs J.Russell & Miss M.Santangelo ....walk over

45. Miss B.Stewart (AUS) & Miss S.Stosur (AUS) ....
46. Miss D.Chladkova (CZE) & Miss H.Nagyova (SVK) ...
    Miss B.Stewart & Miss S.Stosur 6/3 6/4

47. Miss J.Craybas (USA) & Miss M.Weingartner (GER) .
48. Miss M.Navratilova (USA) & Miss L.M.Raymond (USA) [3]
    Miss M.Navratilova & Miss L.M.Raymond [3] 6/2 6/4

    Miss M.Navratilova & Miss L.M.Raymond [3] 6/3 6/1

    Miss M.Navratilova & Miss L.M.Raymond [3] 7/5 6/3

    Mrs L.Huber & Miss A.Sugiyama [5] ....7/6(4) 7/5

49. Mrs L.Huber (RSA) & Miss A.Sugiyama (JPN) ......[5]
(W) 50. Miss H.Crook (GBR) & Miss A.Hawkins (GBR) ......
    Mrs L.Huber & Miss A.Sugiyama [5] 6/1 7/5

(W) 51. Miss H.Collin (GBR) & Miss A.Keothavong (GBR) ....
52. Miss J.Lehnhoff (USA) & Miss B.Mattek (USA) ......
    Miss J.Lehnhoff & Miss B.Mattek 6/3 6/0

    Mrs L.Huber & Miss A.Sugiyama [5] 6/3 6/4

53. Miss Z.Gubacsi (HUN) & Miss K.Nagy (HUN) ....
54. Miss Z.Yan (CHN) & Miss J.Zheng (CHN) ....
    Miss Z.Yan & Miss J.Zheng ....7/6(10) 7/6(5)

55. Miss A.Serra Zanetti (ITA) & Miss A.Serra Zanetti (ITA)
56. Miss M.Casanova (SUI) & Miss N.J.Pratt (AUS) ....[9]
    Miss M.Casanova & Miss N.J.Pratt [9] 6/1 6/2

    Miss Z.Yan & Miss J.Zheng 6/4 4/6 6/4

    Mrs L.Huber & Miss A.Sugiyama [5] 6/1 7/5

57. Miss E.Gagliardi (SUI) & Miss R.Vinci (ITA) ....[16]
(Q) 58. Miss M-R.Jeon (KOR) & Miss Y.Yoshida (JPN) ......
    Miss E.Gagliardi & Miss R.Vinci [16] 3/6 7/5 6/4

59. Miss Y.Beygelzimer (UKR) & Miss T.Poutchek (BLR) .
(L) 60. Miss C.Curran (IRL) & Miss J.O'Donoghue (GBR) ....
    Miss Y.Beygelzimer & Miss T.Poutchek 6/4

    Miss E.Gagliardi & Miss R.Vinci [16] 6/3 6/3

61. Miss N.Dechy (FRA) & Miss D.Hantuchova (SVK) ....
(W) 62. Miss S.Borwell (GBR) & Miss E.Webley-Smith (GBR)
    Miss N.Dechy & Miss D.Hantuchova 6/4 6/1

63. Miss Y.J.Cho (KOR) & Miss L.Granville (USA) ....
64. Miss S.Kuznetsova (RUS) & Miss E.Likhovtseva (RUS) [2]
    Miss S.Kuznetsova & Miss E.Likhovtseva [2] 6/1 6/3

    Miss S.Kuznetsova & Miss E.Likhovtseva [2] 6/3 6/2

    Miss S.Kuznetsova & Miss E.Likhovtseva [2] 2/6 6/3 6/2

    Mrs L.Huber & Miss A.Sugiyama [5] ....7/6(0) 6/3

Quarter-Final / Semi-Final / Final results:

Miss V.Ruano Pascual & Miss P.Suarez [1]

Miss C.Black & Miss R.P.Stubbs [6] ....7/6(7) 4/6 6/4

Mrs L.Huber & Miss A.Sugiyama [5]

Miss C.Black & Miss R.P.Stubbs [6] ....6/3 7/6(5)

Heavy type denotes seeded players. The figure in brackets against names denotes the order in which they have been seeded.
(W) = Wild card. (Q) = Qualifier. (L) = Lucky loser.
The matches are the best of three sets

THE MIXED DOUBLES CHAMPIONSHIP

Holders: L Paes and Miss M Navratilova

The winners become the holders, for the year only, of the CHALLENGE CUP presented by the family of the late Mr S.H. SMITH. The winners receive silver replicas of the Challenge Cup. A silver salver is presented to each of the runners-up and a bronze medal to each defeated semi-finalist.

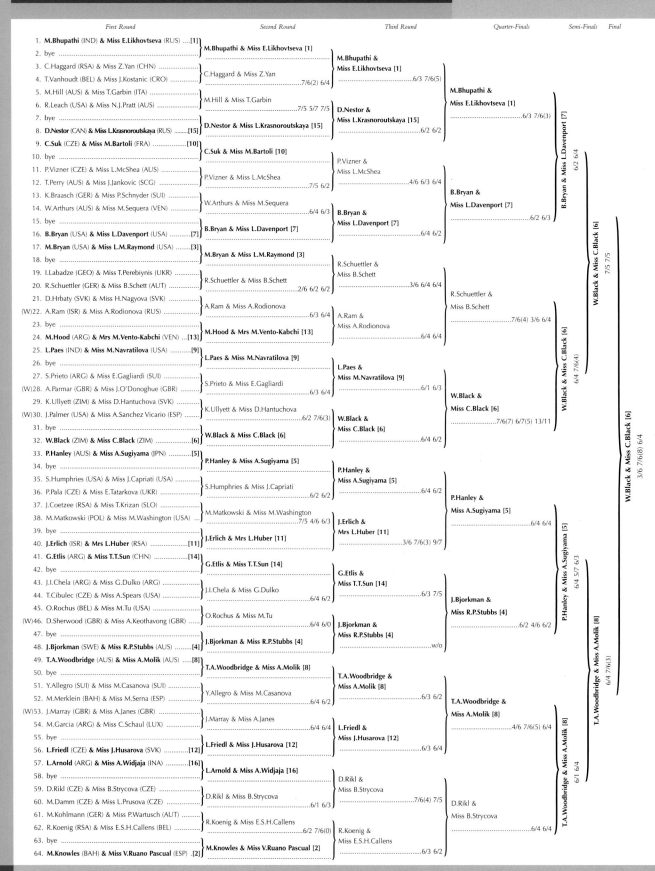

First Round	Second Round	Third Round	Quarter-Finals	Semi-Finals	Final

1. **M.Bhupathi** (IND) & **Miss E.Likhovtseva** (RUS) ....[1]
2. bye
   — M.Bhupathi & Miss E.Likhovtseva [1]
3. C.Haggard (RSA) & Miss Z.Yan (CHN)
4. T.Vanhoudt (BEL) & Miss J.Kostanic (CRO)
   — C.Haggard & Miss Z.Yan ....7/6(2) 6/4
   — M.Bhupathi & Miss E.Likhovtseva [1] ....6/3 7/6(5)
5. M.Hill (AUS) & Miss T.Garbin (ITA)
6. R.Leach (USA) & Miss N.J.Pratt (AUS)
   — M.Hill & Miss T.Garbin 7/5 5/7 7/5
7. bye
8. **D.Nestor** (CAN) & **Miss L.Krasnoroutskaya** (RUS) ....[15]
   — D.Nestor & Miss L.Krasnoroutskaya [15] 6/2 6/2
   — D.Nestor & Miss L.Krasnoroutskaya [15]
   — M.Bhupathi & Miss E.Likhovtseva [1] ....6/3 7/6(3)
9. **C.Suk** (CZE) & **Miss M.Bartoli** (FRA) ....[10]
10. bye
    — C.Suk & Miss M.Bartoli [10]
11. P.Vizner (CZE) & Miss L.McShea (AUS)
12. T.Perry (AUS) & Miss J.Jankovic (SCG)
    — P.Vizner & Miss L.McShea 7/5 6/2
    — P.Vizner & Miss L.McShea 4/6 6/3 6/4
13. K.Braasch (GER) & Miss P.Schnyder (SUI)
14. W.Arthurs (AUS) & Miss M.Sequera (VEN)
    — W.Arthurs & Miss M.Sequera 6/4 6/3
    — B.Bryan & Miss L.Davenport [7]
15. bye
16. **B.Bryan** (USA) & **Miss L.Davenport** (USA) ....[7]
    — B.Bryan & Miss L.Davenport [7] 6/4 6/2
    — B.Bryan & Miss L.Davenport [7] 6/2 6/3
    — B.Bryan & Miss L.Davenport [7] 6/2 6/4
17. **M.Bryan** (USA) & **Miss L.M.Raymond** (USA) ....[3]
18. bye
    — M.Bryan & Miss L.M.Raymond [3]
19. I.Labadze (GEO) & Miss T.Perebiynis (UKR)
20. R.Schuettler (GER) & Miss B.Schett (AUT)
    — R.Schuettler & Miss B.Schett 2/6 6/2 6/2
    — R.Schuettler & Miss B.Schett 3/6 6/4 6/4
21. D.Hrbaty (SVK) & Miss H.Nagyova (SVK)
(W)22. A.Ram (ISR) & Miss A.Rodionova (RUS)
    — A.Ram & Miss A.Rodionova 6/3 6/4
    — A.Ram & Miss A.Rodionova 6/4 6/4
23. bye
24. M.Hood (ARG) & Mrs M.Vento-Kabchi (VEN) ...[13]
    — M.Hood & Mrs M.Vento-Kabchi [13]
    — R.Schuettler & Miss B.Schett ....7/6(4) 3/6 6/4
25. **L.Paes** (IND) & **Miss M.Navratilova** (USA) ....[9]
26. bye
    — L.Paes & Miss M.Navratilova [9]
27. S.Prieto (ARG) & Miss E.Gagliardi (SUI)
(W)28. A.Parmar (GBR) & Miss J.O'Donoghue (GBR)
    — S.Prieto & Miss E.Gagliardi 6/3 6/4
    — L.Paes & Miss M.Navratilova [9] 6/1 6/3
29. K.Ullyett (ZIM) & Miss D.Hantuchova (SVK)
(W)30. J.Palmer (USA) & Miss A.Sanchez Vicario (ESP)
    — K.Ullyett & Miss D.Hantuchova ....6/2 7/6(3)
    — W.Black & Miss C.Black [6]
31. bye
32. **W.Black** (ZIM) & **Miss C.Black** (ZIM) ....[6]
    — W.Black & Miss C.Black [6] 6/4 6/2
    — W.Black & Miss C.Black [6] ....7/6(7) 6/7(5) 13/11
    — W.Black & Miss C.Black [6] ....6/4 7/6(4)
33. **P.Hanley** (AUS) & **Miss A.Sugiyama** (JPN) ....[5]
34. bye
    — P.Hanley & Miss A.Sugiyama [5]
35. S.Humphries (USA) & Miss J.Capriati (USA)
36. P.Pala (CZE) & Miss E.Tatarkova (UKR)
    — S.Humphries & Miss J.Capriati 6/2 6/2
    — P.Hanley & Miss A.Sugiyama [5] 6/4 6/2
37. J.Coetzee (RSA) & Miss T.Krizan (SLO)
38. M.Matkowski (POL) & Miss M.Washington (USA)
    — M.Matkowski & Miss M.Washington 7/5 4/6 6/3
    — J.Erlich & Mrs L.Huber [11]
39. bye
40. **J.Erlich** (ISR) & **Mrs L.Huber** (RSA) ....[11]
    — J.Erlich & Mrs L.Huber [11] ....3/6 7/6(3) 9/7
    — P.Hanley & Miss A.Sugiyama [5] 6/4 6/4
41. **G.Etlis** (ARG) & **Miss T.T.Sun** (CHN) ....[14]
42. bye
    — G.Etlis & Miss T.T.Sun [14]
43. J.I.Chela (ARG) & Miss G.Dulko (ARG)
44. T.Cibulec (CZE) & Miss A.Spears (USA)
    — J.I.Chela & Miss G.Dulko 6/4 6/2
    — G.Etlis & Miss T.T.Sun [14] 6/3 7/5
45. O.Rochus (BEL) & Miss M.Tu (USA)
(W)46. D.Sherwood (GBR) & Miss A.Keothavong (GBR)
    — O.Rochus & Miss M.Tu 6/4 6/0
    — J.Bjorkman & Miss R.P.Stubbs [4]
47. bye
48. **J.Bjorkman** (SWE) & **Miss R.P.Stubbs** (AUS) ....[4]
    — J.Bjorkman & Miss R.P.Stubbs [4]
    — J.Bjorkman & Miss R.P.Stubbs [4] ....w/o
    — J.Bjorkman & Miss R.P.Stubbs [4] 6/2 4/6 6/2
49. **T.A.Woodbridge** (AUS) & **Miss A.Molik** (AUS) ....[8]
50. bye
    — T.A.Woodbridge & Miss A.Molik [8]
51. Y.Allegro (SUI) & Miss M.Casanova (SUI)
52. M.Merklein (BAH) & Miss M.Serna (ESP)
    — Y.Allegro & Miss M.Casanova 6/4 6/2
    — T.A.Woodbridge & Miss A.Molik [8] 6/3 6/2
(W)53. J.Marray (GBR) & Miss A.Janes (GBR)
54. M.Garcia (ARG) & Miss C.Schaul (LUX)
    — J.Marray & Miss A.Janes 6/4 6/4
    — L.Friedl & Miss J.Husarova [12]
55. bye
56. **L.Friedl** (CZE) & **Miss J.Husarova** (SVK) ....[12]
    — L.Friedl & Miss J.Husarova [12]
    — L.Friedl & Miss J.Husarova [12] 6/3 6/4
    — T.A.Woodbridge & Miss A.Molik [8] ....4/6 7/6(5) 6/4
57. **L.Arnold** (ARG) & **Miss A.Widjaja** (INA) ....[16]
58. bye
    — L.Arnold & Miss A.Widjaja [16]
59. D.Rikl (CZE) & Miss B.Strycova (CZE)
60. M.Damm (CZE) & Miss L.Prusova (CZE)
    — D.Rikl & Miss B.Strycova 6/1 6/3
    — D.Rikl & Miss B.Strycova ....7/6(4) 7/5
61. M.Kohlmann (GER) & Miss P.Wartusch (AUT)
62. R.Koenig (RSA) & Miss E.S.H.Callens (BEL)
    — R.Koenig & Miss E.S.H.Callens ....6/2 7/6(0)
    — R.Koenig & Miss E.S.H.Callens 6/4 6/4
63. bye
64. **M.Knowles** (BAH) & **Miss V.Ruano Pascual** (ESP) .[2]
    — M.Knowles & Miss V.Ruano Pascual [2] 6/3 6/2
    — R.Koenig & Miss E.S.H.Callens 6/3 6/4

Quarter-Finals / Semi-Finals / Final:

M.Bhupathi & Miss E.Likhovtseva [1]
B.Bryan & Miss L.Davenport [7]
R.Schuettler & Miss B.Schett
W.Black & Miss C.Black [6]
P.Hanley & Miss A.Sugiyama [5]
J.Bjorkman & Miss R.P.Stubbs [4]
T.A.Woodbridge & Miss A.Molik [8]
D.Rikl & Miss B.Strycova

B.Bryan & Miss L.Davenport [7] 6/2 6/4
W.Black & Miss C.Black [6] ....6/4 7/6(4)
P.Hanley & Miss A.Sugiyama [5] 6/4 5/7 6/3
T.A.Woodbridge & Miss A.Molik [8] 6/1 6/4

W.Black & Miss C.Black [6] 7/5 7/5
T.A.Woodbridge & Miss A.Molik [8] ....6/4 7/6(3)

W.Black & Miss C.Black [6] ....3/6 7/6(8) 6/4

Heavy type denotes seeded players. The figure in brackets against names denotes the order in which they have been seeded.
(W) = Wild card. (Q) = Qualifier. (L) = Lucky loser.
The matches are the best of three sets

THE 35 AND OVER GENTLEMEN'S INVITATION DOUBLES

Holders: M J Bates and N A Fulwood

The winners become the holders, for the year only, of a Cup presented by The All England Lawn Tennis and Croquet Club. The winners receive miniature silver salvers. A silver medal is presented to each of the runners-up.

GROUP A

	C. Pioline (FRA) and R. Seguso (USA)	R. Bergh (SWE) and D. Sapsford (GBR)	L. Jensen (USA) and M. Jensen (USA)	J. Nystrom (SWE) and M. Pernfors (SWE)	WINS	LOSSES
C. Pioline (FRA) and R. Seguso (USA)		6/7(5) 6/4 6/2 W	3/6 6/7(5) L	6/3 6/4 W	2	1
R. Bergh (SWE) and D. Sapsford (GBR)	7/6(5) 4/6 2/6 L		6/2 7/6(2) W	6/3 7/6(4) W	2	1
L. Jensen (USA) and M. Jensen (USA)	6/3 7/6(5) W	2/6 6/7(2) L		4/6 6/1 3/6 L	1	2
J. Nystrom (SWE) and M. Pernfors (SWE)	3/6 4/6 L	3/6 6/7(4) L	6/4 1/6 6/3 W		1	2

GROUP B

	J.B. Fitzgerald (AUS) and W. Masur (AUS)	G.W. Donnelly (USA) and S. Zivojinovic (YUG)	A. Jarryd (SWE) and H. Leconte (FRA)	S. Davis (USA) and D. Pate (USA)	WINS	LOSSES
J.B. Fitzgerald (AUS) and W. Masur (AUS)		7/5 7/5 W	4/6 5/7 L	3/6 2/6 L	1	2
G.W. Donnelly (USA) and S. Zivojinovic (YUG)	5/7 5/7 L		2/6 1/6 L	2/6 4/6 L	0	3
A. Jarryd (SWE) and H. Leconte (FRA)	6/4 7/5 W	6/2 6/1 W		6/7(5) 6/4 3/6 L	2	1
S. Davis (USA) and D. Pate (USA)	6/3 6/2 W	6/2 6/4 W	7/6(5) 4/6 6/3 W		3	0

GROUP C

	S. Casal (ESP) and E. Sanchez (ESP)	J. Frana (ARG) and L. Lavalle (MEX)	P. Galbraith (USA) and S. Melville (USA)	T-J. Middleton (USA) and D. Wheaton (USA)	WINS	LOSSES
S. Casal (ESP) and E. Sanchez (ESP)		6/2 6/0 W	3/6 7/5 6/4 W	3/6 4/6 L	2	1
J. Frana (ARG) and L. Lavalle (MEX)	2/6 0/6 L		5/7 6/7(6) L	3/6 2/6 L	0	3
P. Galbraith (USA) and S. Melville (USA)	6/3 5/7 4/6 L	7/5 7/6(6) W		7/6(3) 2/6 11/13 L	1	2
T-J. Middleton (USA) and D. Wheaton (USA)	6/3 6/4 W	6/3 6/2 W	6/7(3) 6/2 13/11 W		3	0

GROUP D

	D. Rostagno (USA) and L. Shiras (USA)	N. Broad (GBR) and P. Hand (GBR)	M.J. Bates (GBR) and M. Kratzmann (AUS)	P. Aldrich (RSA) and D. Visser (RSA)	WINS	LOSSES
D. Rostagno (USA) and L. Shiras (USA)		2/6 2/6 L	4/6 4/6 L	7/5 6/2 W	1	2
N. Broad (GBR) and P. Hand (GBR)	6/2 6/2 W		7/6(5) 6/2 W	4/6 6/4 3/6 L	2	1
M.J. Bates (GBR) and M. Kratzmann (AUS)	6/4 6/4 W	6/7(5) 2/6 L		6/4 6/4 W	2	1
P. Aldrich (RSA) and D. Visser (RSA)	5/7 2/6 L	6/4 4/6 6/3 W	4/6 4/6 L		1	2

SEMI-FINAL and FINAL

- C. Pioline (FRA) and R. Seguso (USA)
- S. Davis (USA) and D. Pate (USA)
  - Semi-final: C. Pioline (FRA) and R. Seguso (USA) 6/7(4) 6/4 6/4
- T-J. Middleton (USA) and D. Wheaton (USA)
- N. Broad (GBR) and P. Hand (GBR)
  - Semi-final: T-J. Middleton (USA) and D. Wheaton (USA) 6/3 4/6 6/2

FINAL: T-J. Middleton (USA) and D. Wheaton (USA) beat C. Pioline (FRA) and R. Seguso (USA) 4/6 6/1 6/1

This event is played on a 'round robin' basis. Sixteen invited pairs are divided into four groups and each pair in each group plays the others. The pairs winning most matches are the winners of their respective groups and play semi-final and final rounds as indicated above. If matches should be equal in any group, the head-to-head result between the two pairs with the same number of wins determines the winning pair of the group. Heavy type denotes seeded players. **The matches are the best of three sets.** The tie break will operate at six games all in the first two sets.

THE 45 AND OVER GENTLEMEN'S INVITATION DOUBLES

Holders: K Curren and J Kriek

The winners become the holders, for the year only, of a Cup presented by The All England Lawn Tennis and Croquet Club. The winners receive miniature silver salvers. A silver medal is presented to each of the runners-up.

First Round	Quarter-Finals	Semi-Finals	Final
1. K.Curren (USA) & J.Kriek (USA) [1]	K.Curren & J.Kriek [1]		
2. J.G.Alexander (AUS) & P.Dent (AUS)	7/6(4) 6/2	K.Curren & J.Kriek [1]	
3. J.D.Newcombe (AUS) & A.D.Roche (AUS)	S.R.Smith & G.Vilas		
4. S.R.Smith (USA) & G.Vilas (ARG)	6/2 6/3	6/4 6/2	
5. M.Bahrami (IRI) & G.Mayer (USA) [4]	M.Bahrami & G.Mayer [4]		K.Curren & J.Kriek [1]
6. J.W.Feaver (GBR) & J.M.Lloyd (GBR)	6/3 6/2	M.Bahrami & G.Mayer [4]	4/6 7/6(6) 13/11
7. C.Dowdeswell (GBR) & R.Drysdale (GBR)	C.Dowdeswell & R.Drysdale		
8. A.Amritraj (IND) & V.Amritraj (IND)	1/6 6/1 12/10	6/3 6/4	
9. O.K.Davidson (AUS) & A.Stone (AUS)	R.J.Frawley & P.B.McNamara		
10. R.J.Frawley (AUS) & P.B.McNamara (AUS)	6/1 6/2	H.Guenthardt & B.Taroczy [3]	
11. T.R.Gullikson (USA) & R.L.Stockton (USA)	H.Guenthardt & B.Taroczy [3]		
12. H.Guenthardt (SUI) & B.Taroczy (HUN) [3]	7/5 7/6(5)	6/3 6/2	
13. I.Nastase (ROM) & T.S.Okker (NED)	R.L.Case & G.Masters		H.Guenthardt & B.Taroczy [3]
14. R.L.Case (AUS) & G.Masters (AUS)	6/7(4) 7/6(3) 6/3	P.Fleming & A.A.Mayer [2]	7/6(4) 6/1
15. B.E.Gottfried (USA) & R.Ramirez (MEX)	P.Fleming & A.A.Mayer [2]		
16. P.Fleming (USA) & A.A.Mayer (USA) [2]	6/3 6/2	w/o	

Winner: K.Curren & J.Kriek [1] 4/6 6/1 6/4

153

Heavy type denotes seeded players. The figure in brackets against names denotes the order in which they have been seeded. **The matches are the best of three sets** The tie break will operate at six games all in the first two sets.

THE 35 AND OVER LADIES' INVITATION DOUBLES

Holders: Miss I Kloss and Miss K Rinaldi

The winners become the holders, for the year only, of a Cup presented by The All England Lawn Tennis and Croquet Club. The winners receive miniature Cups. A silver medal is presented to each of the runners-up.

GROUP A	Miss I. Kloss (RSA) and Mrs P.D. Smylie (AUS)	Miss K. Adams (USA) and Miss A. Smith (USA)	Miss J.M. Durie (GBR) and Miss H. Sukova (CZE)	Miss C. Lindqvist (SWE) and Miss L. McNeil (USA)	WINS	LOSSES
Miss I. Kloss (RSA) and Mrs P.D. Smylie (AUS)		4/6 2/6 L	5/7 7/5 3/6 L	6/7(4) 1/6 L	0	3
Miss K. Adams (USA) and Miss A. Smith (USA)	6/4 6/2 W		1/6 6/2 6/8 L	7/5 4/6 7/9 L	1	2
Miss J.M. Durie (GBR) and Miss H. Sukova (CZE)	7/5 5/7 6/3 W	6/1 2/6 8/6 W		6/3 6/3 W	3	0
Miss C. Lindqvist (SWE) and Miss L. McNeil (USA)	7/6(4) 6/1 W	5/7 6/4 9/7 W	3/6 3/6 L		2	0

GROUP B	Miss G. Fernandez (USA) and Mrs R.D. Nideffer (RSA)	Mrs G. Magers (USA) and Miss W.M. Turnbull (AUS)	Mrs C. Bassett-Seguso (USA) and Miss H. Mandlikova (AUS)	Miss M. Jausovec (SLO) and Miss J. Novotna (CZE)	WINS	LOSSES
Miss G. Fernandez (USA) and Mrs R.D. Nideffer (RSA)		6/1 6/0 W	6/2 6/0 W	3/6 6/4 8/10 L	2	1
Mrs G. Magers (USA) and Miss W.M. Turnbull (AUS)	1/6 0/6 L		6/1 6/1 W	4/6 4/6 L	1	2
Mrs C. Bassett-Seguso (USA) and Miss H. Mandlikova (AUS)	2/6 0/6 L	1/6 1/6 L		1/6 0/6 L	0	3
Miss M. Jausovec (SLO) and Miss J. Novotna (CZE)	6/3 4/6 10/8 W	6/4 6/4 W	6/1 6/0 W		3	0

FINAL

Miss J.M. Durie (GBR) and Miss H. Sukova (CZE)
Miss M. Jausovec (SLO) and Miss J. Novotna (CZE)
Miss M. Jausovec (SLO) and Miss J. Novotna (CZE) 1/6 7/5 6/1

This event is played on a 'round robin' basis. Eight invited pairs are divided into two groups and each pair in each group plays the others. The pairs winning most matches are the winners of their respective groups and play a final round as indicated above. If matches should be equal in any group, the head-to-head result between the two pairs with the same number of wins determines the winning pair of the group.

Heavy type denotes seeded players.
The matches are the best of three sets

ALPHABETICAL LIST – 35 & OVER EVENTS

GENTLEMEN

Aldrich P. *(South Africa)*
Bates M.J. *(Great Britain)*
Bergh R. *(Sweden)*
Broad N. *(Great Britain)*
Casal S. *(Spain)*
Davis S. *(USA)*
Donnelly G.W. *(USA)*
Fitzgerald J.B. *(Australia)*

Frana J. *(Argentina)*
Galbraith P. *(USA)*
Hand P. *(Great Britain)*
Jarryd A. *(Sweden)*
Jensen L. *(USA)*
Jensen M. *(USA)*
Kratzmann M. *(Australia)*
Lavalle L. *(Mexico)*

Leconte H. *(France)*
Masur W. *(Australia)*
Melville S. *(USA)*
Middleton T.J. *(USA)*
Nystrom J. *(Sweden)*
Pate D. *(USA)*
Pernfors M. *(Sweden)*
Pioline C *(France)*

Rostagno D. *(USA)*
Sanchez E. *(Spain)*
Sapsford D. *(Great Britain)*
Seguso R. *(USA)*
Shiras L. *(USA)*
Wheaton D. *(USA)*
Visser D. *(South Africa)*
Zivojinovic S. *(Yugoslavia)*

LADIES

Adams Miss K. *(USA)*
Bassett-Seguso Mrs C. *(USA)*
Durie Miss J.M. *(Great Britain)*
Fernandez Miss G. *(USA)*

Jausovec Miss M. *(Slovenia)*
Kloss Miss I. *(South Africa)*
Lindqvist Miss C. *(Sweden)*
Magers Mrs G. *(USA)*

Mandlikova Miss H. *(Australia)*
McNeil Miss L. *(USA)*
Nideffer Mrs R.D. *(South Africa)*
Novotna Miss J. *(Czech Republic)*

Smith Miss A. *(USA)*
Smylie Mrs P.D. *(Australia)*
Sukova Miss H. *(Czech Republic)*
Turnbull Miss W.M. *(Australia)*

ALPHABETICAL LIST – 45 & OVER EVENT

GENTLEMEN

Alexander J.G. *(Australia)*
Amrittraj A. *(India)*
Amrittraj V. *(India)*
Bahrami M. *(Iran)*
Case R.L. *(Australia)*
Curren K. *(USA)*
Davidson O.K. *(Australia)*
Dent P. *(Australia)*

Dowdeswell C. *(Great Britain)*
Drysdale R. *(Great Britain)*
Feaver J.W. *(Great Britain)*
Fleming P. *(USA)*
Frawley R.J. *(Australia)*
Gottfried B.E. *(USA)*
Guenthardt H. *(Switzerland)*
Gullikson T.R. *(USA)*

Kriek J. *(USA)*
Lloyd J.M. *(Great Britain)*
Masters G. *(Australia)*
Mayer A. *(USA)*
Mayer G. *(USA)*
McNamara P.B. *(Australia)*
Nastase I. *(Romania)*
Newcombe J.D. *(Australia)*

Okker T.S. *(Netherlands)*
Ramirez R. *(Mexico)*
Roche A.D. *(Australia)*
Smith S.R. *(USA)*
Stockton R.L. *(USA)*
Stone A. *(Australia)*
Taroczy B. *(Hungary)*
Vilas G. *(Argentina)*

THE BOYS' SINGLES CHAMPIONSHIP

Holder: F Mergea

For both the Boys' Singles *and* the Boys' Doubles Championships, the winners become the holders, for the year only, of a Cup presented by The All England Lawn Tennis and Croquet Club. The winners each receive a miniature Cup and the runners-up receive mementoes.

First Round		Second Round	Third Round	Quarter-Finals	Semi-Finals	Final

1. **Monfils, Gael [1]** ....(FRA) — G.Monfils [1] .... 7/6(2) 6/4
2. Rushby, Tom ....(GBR)
3. Simmonds, Phillip ....(USA) — M.Ziadi .... 7/6(5) 7/6(7)
4. Ziadi, Mehdi ....(MAR)
(W) 5. Baker, Jack ....(GBR) — J.Paukku 6/2 6/4
(Q) 6. Paukku, Juho ....(FIN)
(Q) 7. Ouellette, Greg ....(USA) — R.De Rijke [16] 3/6 6/3 6/4
8. **De Rijke, Remko [16]** ....(NED)
9. **Rastogi, Karan [12]** ....(IND) — G.D.Jones 6/4 6/4
10. Jones, G.D. ....(NZL)
11. Alcaide-Justell, Guillermo ....(ESP) — G.Alcaide-Justell .... 3/1 Ret'd.
12. Thron, Aljoscha ....(GER)
13. Amado, Juan Pablo ....(ARG) — J.P.Amado 6/1 3/6 6/1
(W) 14. Khatib, Faris ....(GBR)
15. Arnaboldi, Andrea ....(ITA) — B.Evans [7] 6/2 6/0
16. **Evans, Brendan [7]** ....(USA)
17. **Capkovic, Kamil [4]** ....(SVK) — K.Capkovic [4] 6/3 6/2
18. Bellucci, Thomaz ....(BRA)
(Q) 19. Anderson, Kevin ....(RSA) — K.Anderson 6/4 3/6 6/1
20. Kerley, Joel ....(AUS)
21. Baker, Jamie ....(GBR) — Jm.Baker 6/2 6/0
(W) 22. Leong, Michael ....(SOL)
23. Bubka, Sergei ....(UKR) — S.Bubka 7/5 4/6 6/0
24. **Oudsema, Scott [14]** ....(USA)
25. **Kim, Sun-Yong Jr. [10]** ....(KOR) — J.Chardy 6/1 7/5
(Q) 26. Chardy, Jeremy ....(FRA)
(W) 27. Brown, Matthew ....(GBR) — V.Visak 6/2 6/4
28. Visak, Vilim ....(CRO)
(W) 29. Young, Donald ....(USA) — D.Young 3/6 6/2 6/1
30. Haase, Robin ....(NED)
31. Murray, Jamie ....(GBR) — S.Rieschick [8] 6/4 4/6 6/1
32. **Rieschick, Sebastian [8]** ....(GER)
33. **Kuznetsov, Alex [5]** ....(USA) — A.Kuznetsov [5] .... 6/2 7/6(4)
34. Muller, Daniel ....(GER)
(W) 35. Desein, Niels ....(BEL) — N.Desein 6/3 6/2
(W) 36. Wire, Richard ....(GBR)
37. Lacko, Lukas ....(SVK) — R.Herold .... 6/7(5) 6/4 6/4
(Q) 38. Herold, Roman ....(GER)
39. Ward, William ....(NZL) — W.Ward 2/6 6/2 6/4
40. **Andujar-Alba, Pablo [9]** ....(ESP)
41. **Van Keulen, Coen [15]** ....(NED) — T.Neilly 6/4 6/4
42. Neilly, Timothy ....(GBR)
43. Arevalo Gonzalez, Rafael ....(ESA) — M.Kasiri ...... 6/0 7/6(17)
44. Kasiri, Miles ....(GBR)
45. Yi, Chu-Huan ....(TPE) — C-H.Yi 6/1 3/6 6/1
46. Sharan, Divij ....(IND)
47. Ferguson, Lachlan ....(AUS) — J.Ouanna [3] .... 7/6(4) 6/2
48. **Ouanna, Josselin [3]** ....(FRA)
49. **Zverev, Mihail [6]** ....(GER) — M.Zverev [6] 6/3 6/4
(L) 50. Oswald, Philipp ....(AUT)
(Q) 51. Fujii, Takanobu ....(JPN) — M.Fischer 6/1 6/4
(Q) 52. Fischer, Martin ....(AUT)
53. Del Potro, Juan-Martin ....(ARG) — J-M.Del Potro ...... 6/4 7/6(6)
(W) 54. Cavaday, Nick ....(GBR)
55. Miklusicak, Peter ....(SVK) — S.Jenkins [11] 6/3 6/4
56. **Jenkins, Scoville [11]** ....(USA)
57. **Fognini, Fabio [13]** ....(ITA) — W-S.Jun 6/2 6/3
58. Jun, Woong-Sun ....(KOR)
59. Troicki, Viktor ....(SCG) — V.Troicki .... 6/7(5) 7/6(2) 6/1
60. Liberhan, Tushar ....(IND)
61. Nedovesov, Alexander ....(UKR) — A.Nedovesov 6/3 6/4
62. Mirzadeh, Vahid ....(USA)
(Q) 63. Kryvonos, Mykyta ....(USA) — A.Murray [2] 3/6 6/4 6/2
64. **Murray, Andrew [2]** ....(GBR)

Third Round:
- G.Monfils [1] .... 4/6 7/6(2) 6/2
- R.De Rijke [16] 6/4 6/3
- G.D.Jones 7/5 3/6 6/4
- B.Evans [7] 6/4 6/4
- K.Capkovic [4] 4/6 6/3 8/6
- Jm.Baker .... 6/1 7/6(1)
- J.Chardy 6/1 6/4
- S.Rieschick [8] 6/2 6/4
- N.Desein .... 6/4 7/6(5)
- W.Ward 6/4 7/5
- M.Kasiri 7/5 6/1
- J.Ouanna [3] .... 7/6(1) 6/3
- M.Fischer 1/6 6/2 6/3
- S.Jenkins [11] 6/3 6/4
- W-S.Jun .... 7/6(3) 6/3
- A.Murray [2] 6/2 6/2

Quarter-Finals:
- G.Monfils [1] 6/2 6/4
- B.Evans [7] 6/2 6/1
- Jm.Baker 6/3 6/4
- J.Chardy 6/2 2/6 6/2
- W.Ward 3/6 6/3 6/2
- M.Kasiri 6/3 5/7 7/5
- S.Jenkins [11] .... 7/6(5) 6/3
- W-S.Jun 7/5 6/3

Semi-Finals:
- G.Monfils [1] 7/5 6/2
- J.Chardy ....6/4 7/6(4)
- M.Kasiri 6/4 6/3
- S.Jenkins [11] 6/3 6/3

Final:
- G.Monfils [1] 6/4 6/2
- M.Kasiri 7/6(5) 7/6(3)

G.Monfils [1] 7/5 7/6(6)

THE BOYS' DOUBLES CHAMPIONSHIP

Holders: F Mergea and H Tecau

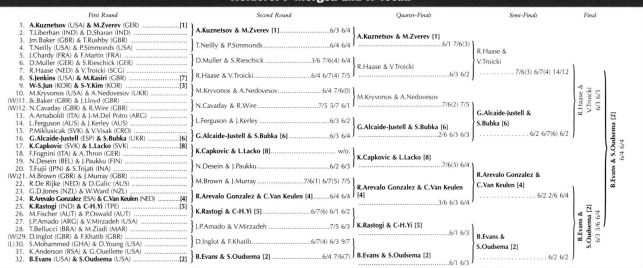

First Round		Second Round	Quarter-Finals	Semi-Finals	Final

1. **A.Kuznetsov (USA) & M.Zverev (GER)** ....[1] — A.Kuznetsov & M.Zverev [1] 6/3 6/4
2. T.Liberhan (IND) & D.Sharan (IND)
3. Jm.Baker (GBR) & T.Rushby (GBR) — T.Neilly & P.Simmonds 6/4 6/4
4. T.Neilly (USA) & P.Simmonds (USA)
5. J.Chardy (FRA) & F.Martin (FRA) — D.Muller & S.Rieschick ....3/6 7/6(4) 6/4
6. D.Muller (GER) & S.Rieschick (GER)
7. R.Haase (NED) & V.Troicki (SCG) — R.Haase & V.Troicki ....6/4 6/7(4) 7/5
8. **S.Jenkins (USA) & M.Kasiri (GBR)** ....[7]
9. **W-S.Jun (KOR) & S-Y.Kim (KOR)** ....[3] — M.Kryvonos & A.Nedovesov ....6/4 7/6(0)
10. M.Kryvonos (USA) & A.Nedovesov (UKR)
(W)11. Jk.Baker (GBR) & J.Lloyd (GBR) — N.Cavaday & R.Wire 7/5 5/7 6/1
(W)12. N.Cavaday (GBR) & R.Wire (GBR)
13. A.Arnaboldi (ITA) & J-M.Del Potro (ARG) — L.Ferguson & J.Kerley 6/3 6/2
14. L.Ferguson (AUS) & J.Kerley (AUS)
15. P.Miklusicak (SVK) & V.Visak (CRO) — G.Alcaide-Justell & S.Bubka [6] 6/3 6/4
16. **G.Alcaide-Justell (ESP) & S.Bubka (UKR)** ....[6]
17. **K.Capkovic (SVK) & L.Lacko (SVK)** ....[8] — K.Capkovic & L.Lacko [8] ....w/o.
18. F.Fognini (ITA) & A.Thron (GER)
19. N.Desein (BEL) & J.Paukku (FIN) — N.Desein & J.Paukku 6/2 6/3
20. T.Fujii (JPN) & S.Trijati (INA)
(W)21. M.Brown (GBR) & J.Murray (GBR) — M.Brown & J.Murray ....7/6(1) 6/7(5) 7/5
22. R.De Rijke (NED) & D.Galic (AUS)
23. G.D.Jones (NZL) & W.Ward (NZL) — R.Arevalo Gonzalez & C.Van Keulen [4] 6/4 6/4
24. **R.Arevalo Gonzalez (ESA) & C.Van Keulen (NED)** ....[4]
25. **K.Rastogi (IND) & C-H.Yi (TPE)** ....[5] — K.Rastogi & C-H.Yi [5] ....6/7(6) 6/1 6/2
26. M.Fischer (AUT) & P.Oswald (AUT)
27. J.P.Amado (ARG) & V.Mirzadeh (USA) — J.P.Amado & V.Mirzadeh 7/5 6/3
28. T.Bellucci (BRA) & M.Ziadi (MAR)
(W)29. D.Inglot (GBR) & F.Khatib (GBR) — D.Inglot & F.Khatib ....6/7(4) 6/3 9/7
(L)30. S.Mohammed (GHA) & D.Young (USA)
31. K.Anderson (RSA) & G.Ouellette (USA) — B.Evans & S.Oudsema [2] ....6/4 7/6(7)
32. **B.Evans (USA) & S.Oudsema (USA)** ....[2]

Quarter-Finals:
- A.Kuznetsov & M.Zverev [1] ....6/1 7/6(3)
- R.Haase & V.Troicki 6/3 6/2
- M.Kryvonos & A.Nedovesov ....7/6(2) 6/3
- G.Alcaide-Justell & S.Bubka [6] 2/6 6/3 6/3
- K.Capkovic & L.Lacko [8] ....7/6(3) 6/4
- R.Arevalo Gonzalez & C.Van Keulen [4] 3/6 6/3 6/4
- K.Rastogi & C-H.Yi [5] 6/1 6/3
- B.Evans & S.Oudsema [2] 6/1 6/3

Semi-Finals:
- R.Haase & V.Troicki ....7/6(3) 6/7(4) 14/12
- G.Alcaide-Justell & S.Bubka [6] ....6/2 7/6(6) 6/2
- R.Arevalo Gonzalez & C.Van Keulen [4] 6/2 2/6 6/4
- B.Evans & S.Oudsema [2] 6/2 6/2

Final:
- R.Haase & V.Troicki 6/3 6/3
- B.Evans & S.Oudsema [2] 6/3 3/6 6/4

B.Evans & S.Oudsema [2] 6/4 6/4

Heavy type denotes seeded players. The figure in brackets against names denotes the order in which they have been seeded.   (W) = Wild card. (Q) = Qualifier. (L) = Lucky loser.

The matches are the best of three sets

THE GIRLS' SINGLES CHAMPIONSHIP

For both the Girls' Singles and the Girls' Doubles Championships, the winners become the holders, for the year only, of a Cup presented by The All England Lawn Tennis and Croquet Club. The winners each receive a miniature Cup and the runners-up receive mementos.

Holder: Miss K Flipkens

First Round	Second Round	Third Round	Quarter-Finals	Semi-Finals	Final
1. Krajicek, Michaela [1].................(NED)	Miss M.Krajicek [1] 6/3 6/1				
2. Szavay, Agnes...........................(HUN)		Miss M.Krajicek [1]			
(L) 3. Thijssen, Nicole.....................(NED)	Miss N.Thijssen ....7/6(3) 6/2	.... 6/1 6/0			
4. Molinero, Florencia ....(ARG)			Miss M.Krajicek [1]		
(Q) 5. Kobak, Elizabeth...................(USA)	Miss E.Kobak 6/3 6/1		........................6/2 6/2		
6. Schnack, Yasmin.......................(USA)		Miss I.Kotkina [15]			
7. Rybarikova, Magdalena.............(SVK)	Miss I.Kotkina [15] 6/1 6/4	.... 7/6(3) 6/3			
8. Kotkina, Irina [15].....................(RUS)				Miss M.Krajicek [1]	
9. Chvojkova, Veronika [12]..........(CZE)	Miss G.Gabba ....6/2 7/6(5)			.................6/1 6/2	
10. Gabba, Giulia ....(ITA)		Miss E.Rodina			
11. Rodina, Evgeniya.....................(RUS)	Miss E.Rodina 6/1 6/0	.... 6/3 6/1			
12. Iyer, Tara ....(IND)			Miss V.Lukic		
(W) 13. Ferguson, Sophie...............(AUS)	Miss S.Ferguson.......6/7(5) 4/6 6/2		..................7/5 6/1		
(W) 14. Grady, Hannah...................(GBR)		Miss V.Lukic			
15. Lukic, Vojislava.......................(SCG)	Miss V.Lukic 0/6 6/3 8/6	.... 6/3 1/6 6/3			
16. Niculescu, Monica [7]..............(ROM)					
17. Peer, Shahar [4].......................(ISR)	Miss S.Peer [4] 6/3 6/2				Miss K.Bondarenko [6]
18. Kulikova, Regina......................(RUS)		Miss S.Peer [4]			7/6(1) 1/6 6/4
(W) 19. Uberoi, Neha.....................(USA)	Miss N.Uberoi 6/2 6/4	.... 6/3 6/2			
20. Jerman, Ana.............................(SLO)			Miss S.Peer [4]		
(Q) 21. Mircic, Teodora..................(SCG)	Miss A.Szatmari 6/4 6/1		..................6/1 6/1		
22. Szatmari, Agnes.......................(ROM)		Miss A.Szatmari			
23. Kramperova, Katerina...............(CZE)	Miss K.Kramperova 6/3 6/4	.... 6/2 6/3			
24. Fuda, Ryoko [14]......................(JPN)				Miss K.Bondarenko [6]	
25. Havartsova, Volha [10].............(BLR)	Miss V.Havartsova [10] 6/4 6/2			.........................6/3 3/6 6/1	
26. Biglmaier, Maraike....................(GER)		Miss V.Havartsova [10]			
27. Hsu, Wen-Hsin.........................(TPE)	Miss E.Grebeniuk ....7/6(4) 4/6 6/2	.... 6/2 6/4			
28. Grebeniuk, Eugenia..................(RUS)			Miss K.Bondarenko [6]		
(Q) 29. Baker, Katharine.................(GBR)	Miss K.Tsang 2/6 6/2 6/2		..................6/2 6/4		
30. Tsang, Katrina..........................(USA)		Miss K.Bondarenko [6]			
(W) 31. O'Brien, Katie....................(GBR)	Miss K.Bondarenko [6] 6/2 6/3	.... 6/0 6/1			
32. Bondarenko, Katerina [6].........(UKR)					
33. Kleybanova, Alisa [8]...............(RUS)	Miss A.Kleybanova [8] 6/1 6/1				
(W) 34. Fakhoury, Lara...................(GBR)		Miss A.Kleybanova [8]			
(Q) 35. Sema, Yurika......................(JPN)	Miss T.Malek 6/4 5/7 6/0	.... 6/1 6/1			
36. Malek, Tatjana..........................(GER)			Miss A.Kleybanova [8]		
37. Verardi, Verdiana......................(ITA)	Miss N.Frankova ....6/3 7/6(6)		..................6/1 6/3		
38. Frankova, Nikola.......................(CZE)		Miss M.Erakovic [11]			
(Q) 39. Kirianova, Ekaterina............(RUS)	Miss M.Erakovic [11]......7/6(2) 6/4	.... 6/4 6/4			
40. Erakovic, Marina [11]...............(NZL)				Miss A.Ivanovic [3]	
41. Gojnea, Madalina [16]..............(ROM)	Miss E.Kosminskaya.........7/5 4/6 6/3			.........................7/6(1) 6/1	
42. Kosminskaya, Ekaterina...........(RUS)		Miss E.Kosminskaya			
(Q) 43. Bobusic, Bojana.................(AUS)	Miss B.Bobusic 1/6 6/2 10/8	.... 6/1 6/2			
(L) 44. Wozniaki, Caroline..............(DEN)			Miss A.Ivanovic [3]		
(Q) 45. Pavlovic, Irena...................(FRA)	Miss I.Pavlovic 6/2 6/0		..................4/6 6/1 6/1		
46. Balda, Estefania.......................(ECU)		Miss A.Ivanovic [3]			
47. Ancic, Sanja............................(CRO)	Miss A.Ivanovic [3] ....5/0 Ret'd.	.... 6/1 6/0			
48. Ivanovic, Ana [3].....................(SCG)					Miss A.Ivanovic [3]
49. Chan, Yung-Jan [5]..................(TPE)	Miss Y-J.Chan [5] 7/5 6/4				6/0 1/6 12/10
(Q) 50. Zubori, Ana-Maria..............(FRA)		Miss A.Wozniak			
51. Wozniak, Aleksandra................(CAN)	Miss A.Wozniak 6/2 6/2	.... 6/4 7/5			
52. Sun, Shengnan.........................(CHN)			Miss V.Azarenka [9]		
53. Kerber, Angelique.....................(GER)	Miss A.Kerber 6/1 7/5		..................5/7 6/4 7/5		
(W) 54. Gullickson, Carly...............(USA)		Miss V.Azarenka [9]			
(W) 55. South, Melanie...................(GBR)	Miss V.Azarenka [9] 6/1 6/3	.... 1/6 7/5 6/3			
56. Azarenka, Viktoria [9]..............(BLR)				Miss V.Azarenka [9]	
57. Kirkland, Jessica [13]...............(USA)	Miss J.Kirkland [13] 6/3 6/2			.........................7/6(4) 7/5	
58. Zec-Peskiric, Masa...................(SLO)		Miss A.Kudryavtseva			
59. Schutte, Ghizela......................(RSA)	Miss A.Kudryavtseva 6/4 6/3	.... 7/5 6/4			
60. Kudryavtseva, Alla...................(RUS)			Miss N.Vaidisova [2]		
61. Juricova, Jana..........................(SVK)	Miss C.Peterzan ....7/6(3) 3/6 6/3		..................7/5 6/2		
(W) 62. Peterzan, Claire..................(GBR)		Miss N.Vaidisova [2]			
63. Thongdach, Pichitta..................(THA)	Miss N.Vaidisova [2] 6/3 6/0	.... 6/2 6/3			
64. Vaidisova, Nicole [2]................(CZE)					

THE GIRLS' DOUBLES CHAMPIONSHIP

Holders: Miss A Kleybanova and Miss S Mirza

First Round	Second Round	Quarter-Finals	Semi-Finals	Final
1. Miss M.Krajicek (NED) & Miss S.Peer (ISR) ....[1]	Miss M.Krajicek & Miss S.Peer [1] 4/6 6/3 9/7			Miss K.Bondarenko [6]
2. Miss N.Frankova (CZE) & Miss A.Szavay (HUN)		Miss M.Krajicek & Miss S.Peer [1]		
3. Miss T.Mircic (SCG) & Miss I.Pavlovic (FRA)	Miss T.Mircic & Miss I.Pavlovic ....6/7(4) 6/3 6/3	................6/3 6/2		
4. Miss G.Schutte (RSA) & Miss A.Szatmari (ROM)			Miss M.Krajicek & Miss S.Peer [1]	
5. Miss E.Kirianova (RUS) & Miss V.Lukic (SCG)	Miss E.Kirianova & Miss V.Lukic 6/2 6/3		....................6/2 6/4	
6. Miss E.Grebeniuk (RUS) & Miss K.Kramperova (CZE)		Miss Y-J.Chan & Miss A.Wozniak [6]		
7. Miss W.Liu (CHN) & Miss S.Zhang (CHN)	Miss Y-J.Chan & Miss A.Wozniak [6] 6/1 6/4	................6/1 6/0		
8. Miss Y-J.Chan (TPE) & Miss A.Wozniak (CAN) ......[6]				
9. Miss V.Azarenka (BLR) & Miss V.Havartsova (BLR) [3]	Miss V.Azarenka & Miss V.Havartsova [3] 6/4 7/5			Miss V.Azarenka & Miss V.Havartsova [3]
10. Miss E.Balda (ECU) & Miss P.Thongdach (THA)		Miss V.Azarenka & Miss V.Havartsova [3]		7/6(3) 6/2
11. Miss E.Kosminskaya (RUS) & Miss E.Makarova (RUS)		................6/2 3/6 6/4		
12. Miss A.Kerber (GER) & Miss T.Malek (GER)	Miss A.Kerber & Miss T.Malek 6/0 6/3		Miss V.Azarenka & Miss V.Havartsova [3]	
13. Miss G.Gabba (ITA) & Miss V.Verardi (ITA)	Miss G.Gabba & Miss V.Verardi 6/2 6/1		....................6/0 6/2	
(W)14. Miss H.Grady (GBR) & Miss C.Peterzan (GBR)		Miss G.Gabba & Miss V.Verardi		
15. Miss Y.Schnack (USA) & Miss K.Tsang (USA)	Miss Y.Schnack & Miss K.Tsang............4/6 6/4 13/11	.... w/o.		
16. Miss W-H.Hsu (TPE) & Miss S-N.Sun (CHN) ....[8]				
17. Miss A.Kleybanova (RUS) & Miss I.Kotkina (RUS) [7]	Miss A.Kleybanova & Miss I.Kotkina [7]......6/0 6/3			Miss V.Azarenka & Miss V.Havartsova [3]
18. Miss M.Zec-Peskiric (SLO) & Miss A.Zubori (FRA)		Miss A.Kleybanova & Miss I.Kotkina [7]		6/4 3/6 6/4
19. Miss B.Jozami (ARG) & Miss F.Molinero (ARG)	Miss B.Jozami & Miss F.Molinero 6/3 6/2	................6/1 6/1		
20. Miss B.Bobusic (AUS) & Miss S.Ferguson (AUS)			Miss M.Erakovic & Miss M.Niculescu [4]	
21. Miss R.Fuda (JPN) & Miss N.Uberoi (USA)	Miss R.Fuda & Miss N.Uberoi 6/3 6/0		....................6/2 6/7(5) 6/0	
(W)22. Miss N.Khan (GBR) & Miss L.Peterzan (GBR)		Miss M.Erakovic & Miss M.Niculescu [4]		
23. Miss L.Giltinan (AUS) & Miss C.Wozniaki (DEN)	Miss M.Erakovic & Miss M.Niculescu [4]....6/1 7/6(5)	................3/6 7/6(2) 6/4		
24. Miss M.Erakovic (NZL) & Miss M.Niculescu (ROM) ....[4]				
25. Miss K.Bondarenko (UKR) & Miss M.Gojnea (ROM) ....[5]	Miss K.Bondarenko & Miss M.Gojnea [5] .3/6 6/0 7/5			Miss V.Chvojkova & Miss N.Vaidisova [2]
26. Miss T.Iyer (IND) & Miss E.Kobak (USA)		Miss K.O'Brien & Miss M.South		
(W)27. Miss K.O'Brien (GBR) & Miss M.South (GBR)	Miss K.O'Brien & Miss M.South 6/3 4/6 6/4	........................7/6(3) 6/3		
28. Miss R.Kulikova (RUS) & Miss E.Rodina (RUS)			Miss V.Chvojkova & Miss N.Vaidisova [2]	
29. Miss Y.Sema (JPN) & Miss N.Thijssen (NED)	Miss Y.Sema & Miss N.Thijssen 6/4 6/4		....................6/1 6/2	
30. Miss J.Juricova (SVK) & Miss M.Rybarikova (SVK)		Miss V.Chvojkova & Miss N.Vaidisova [2]		
(W)31. Miss J.Curtis (GBR) & Miss L.Fakhoury (GBR)	Miss V.Chvojkova & Miss N.Vaidisova [2] 6/1 6/0	...............6/7(2) 6/4 7/5		
32. Miss V.Chvojkova (CZE) & Miss N.Vaidisova (CZE) ....[2]				

Heavy type denotes seeded players. The figure in brackets against names denotes the order in which they have been seeded.
(W) = Wild card. (Q) = Qualifier. (L) = Lucky loser. **The matches are the best of three sets**

Champions and Runners-up

Year	Champion / Runner-up	Year	Champion / Runner-up	Year	Champion / Runner-up	Year	Champion / Runner-up	Year	Champion / Runner-up
1877	S. W. Gore / *W. C. Marshall*	1900	R. F. Doherty / *S. H. Smith*	1927	H. Cochet / *J. Borotra*	* 1956	L. A. Hoad / *K. R. Rosewall*	1980	B. Borg / *J. P. McEnroe*
1878	P. F. Hadow / *S. W. Gore*	1901	A. W. Gore / *R. F. Doherty*	1928	R. Lacoste / *H. Cochet*	1957	L. A. Hoad / *A. J. Cooper*	1981	J. P. McEnroe / *B. Borg*
* 1879	J. T. Hartley / *V. St. L. Goold*	1902	H. L. Doherty / *A. W. Gore*	* 1929	H. Cochet / *J. Borotra*	* 1958	A. J. Cooper / *N. A. Fraser*	1982	J. S. Connors / *J. P. McEnroe*
1880	J. T. Hartley / *H. F. Lawford*	1903	H. L. Doherty / *F. L. Riseley*	1930	W. T. Tilden / *W. Allison*	* 1959	A. Olmedo / *R. Laver*	1983	J. P. McEnroe / *C. J. Lewis*
1881	W. Renshaw / *J. T. Hartley*	1904	H. L. Doherty / *F. L. Riseley*	* 1931	S. B. Wood / *F. X. Shields*	* 1960	N. A. Fraser / *R. Laver*	1984	J. P. McEnroe / *J. S. Connors*
1882	W. Renshaw / *E. Renshaw*	1905	H. L. Doherty / *N. E. Brookes*	1932	H. E. Vines / *H. W. Austin*	1961	R. Laver / *C. R. McKinley*	1985	B. Becker / *K. Curren*
1883	W. Renshaw / *E. Renshaw*	1906	H. L. Doherty / *F. L. Riseley*	1933	J. H. Crawford / *H. E. Vines*	1962	R. Laver / *M. F. Mulligan*	1986	B. Becker / *I. Lendl*
1884	W. Renshaw / *H. F. Lawford*	* 1907	N. E. Brookes / *A. W. Gore*	1934	F. J. Perry / *J. H. Crawford*	* 1963	C. R. McKinley / *F. S. Stolle*	1987	P. Cash / *I. Lendl*
1885	W. Renshaw / *H. F. Lawford*	* 1908	A. W. Gore / *H. Roper Barrett*	1935	F. J. Perry / *G. von Cramm*	1964	R. Emerson / *F. S. Stolle*	1988	S. Edberg / *B. Becker*
1886	W. Renshaw / *H. F. Lawford*	1909	A. W. Gore / *M. J. G. Ritchie*	1936	F. J. Perry / *G. von Cramm*	1965	R. Emerson / *F. S. Stolle*	1989	B. Becker / *S. Edberg*
* 1887	H. F. Lawford / *E. Renshaw*	1910	A. F. Wilding / *A. W. Gore*	* 1937	J. D. Budge / *G. von Cramm*	1966	M. Santana / *R. D. Ralston*	1990	S. Edberg / *B. Becker*
1888	E. Renshaw / *H. F. Lawford*	1911	A. F. Wilding / *H. Roper Barrett*	1938	J. D. Budge / *H. W. Austin*	1967	J. D. Newcombe / *W. P. Bungert*	1991	M. Stich / *B. Becker*
1889	W. Renshaw / *E. Renshaw*	1912	A. F. Wilding / *A. W. Gore*	* 1939	R. L. Riggs / *E. T. Cooke*	1968	R. Laver / *A. D. Roche*	1992	A. Agassi / *G. Ivanisevic*
1890	W. J. Hamilton / *W. Renshaw*	1913	A. F. Wilding / *M. E. McLoughlin*	* 1946	Y. Petra / *G. E. Brown*	1969	R. Laver / *J. D. Newcombe*	1993	P. Sampras / *J. Courier*
* 1891	W. Baddeley / *J. Pim*	1914	N. E. Brookes / *A. F. Wilding*	1947	J. Kramer / *T. Brown*	1970	J. D. Newcombe / *K. R. Rosewall*	1994	P. Sampras / *G. Ivanisevic*
1892	W. Baddeley / *J. Pim*	1919	G. L. Patterson / *N. E. Brookes*	* 1948	R. Falkenburg / *J. E. Bromwich*	1971	J. D. Newcombe / *S. R. Smith*	1995	P. Sampras / *B. Becker*
1893	J. Pim / *W. Baddeley*	1920	W. T. Tilden / *G. L. Patterson*	1949	F. R. Schroeder / *J. Drobny*	* 1972	S. R. Smith / *I. Nastase*	1996	R. Krajicek / *M. Washington*
1894	J. Pim / *W. Baddeley*	1921	W. T. Tilden / *B. I. C. Norton*	* 1950	B. Patty / *F. A. Sedgman*	* 1973	J. Kodes / *A. Metreveli*	1997	P. Sampras / *C. Pioline*
* 1895	W. Baddeley / *W. V. Eaves*	*† 1922	G. L. Patterson / *R. Lycett*	1951	R. Savitt / *K. McGregor*	1974	J. S. Connors / *K. R. Rosewall*	1998	P. Sampras / *G. Ivanisevic*
1896	H. S. Mahony / *W. Baddeley*	* 1923	W. M. Johnston / *F. T. Hunter*	1952	F. A. Sedgman / *J. Drobny*	1975	A. R. Ashe / *J. S. Connors*	1999	P. Sampras / *A. Agassi*
1897	R. F. Doherty / *H. S. Mahony*	* 1924	J. Borotra / *R. Lacoste*	* 1953	V. Seixas / *K. Nielsen*	1976	B. Borg / *I. Nastase*	2000	P. Sampras / *P. Rafter*
1898	R. F. Doherty / *H. L. Doherty*	1925	R. Lacoste / *J. Borotra*	1954	J. Drobny / *K. R. Rosewall*	1977	B. Borg / *J. S. Connors*	2001	G. Ivanisevic / *P. Rafter*
1899	R. F. Doherty / *A. W. Gore*	* 1926	J. Borotra / *H. Kinsey*	1955	T. Trabert / *K. Nielsen*	1978	B. Borg / *J. S. Connors*	2002	L. Hewitt / *D. Nalbandian*
						1979	B. Borg / *R. Tanner*	2003	R. Federer / *M. Philippoussis*

NOTE: For the years 1913, 1914 and 1919-23 inclusive the Championship Roll includes the 'World's Championship on Grass' granted to The Lawn Tennis Association by The International Lawn Tennis Federation. This title was then abolished and commencing in 1924 they became The Official Lawn Tennis Championships recognised by The International Lawn Tennis Federation. Prior to 1922 the holders in the singles events and the gentlemen's doubles did not compete in The Championships but met the winners of these events in the Challenge Rounds.
† Challenge Round abolished; holders subsequently played through. *The holder did not defend the title.

1884	Miss M. Watson *Miss L. Watson*	1906	Miss D. K. Douglass *Miss M. Sutton*	★1932	Mrs. F. S. Moody *Miss H. H. Jacobs*	★1959	Miss M. E. Bueno *Miss D. R. Hard*	1980	Mrs. R. Cawley *Mrs. J. M. Lloyd*
1885	Miss M. Watson *Miss B. Bingley*	1907	Miss M. Sutton *Mrs. Lambert Chambers*	1933	Mrs. F. S. Moody *Miss D. E. Round*	1960	Miss M. E. Bueno *Miss S. Reynolds*	★1981	Mrs. J. M. Lloyd *Miss H. Mandlikova*
1886	Miss B. Bingley *Miss M. Watson*	★1908	Mrs. A. Sterry *Miss A. M. Morton*	★1934	Miss D. E. Round *Miss H. H. Jacobs*	★1961	Miss A. Mortimer *Miss C. C. Truman*	1982	Miss M. Navratilova *Mrs. J. M. Lloyd*
1887	Miss L. Dod *Miss B. Bingley*	★1909	Miss D. P. Boothby *Miss A. M. Morton*	1935	Mrs. F. S. Moody *Miss H. H. Jacobs*	1962	Mrs. J. R. Susman *Mrs. V. Sukova*	1983	Miss M. Navratilova *Miss A. Jaeger*
1888	Miss L. Dod *Mrs. G. W. Hillyard*	1910	Mrs. Lambert Chambers *Miss D. P. Boothby*	★1936	Miss H. H. Jacobs *Frau. S. Sperling*	★1963	Miss M. Smith *Miss B. J. Moffitt*	1984	Miss M. Navratilova *Mrs. J. M. Lloyd*
★1889	Mrs. G. W. Hillyard *Miss L. Rice*	1911	Mrs. Lambert Chambers *Miss D. P. Boothby*	1937	Miss D. E. Round *Miss J. Jedrzejowska*	1964	Miss M. E. Bueno *Miss M. Smith*	1985	Miss M. Navratilova *Mrs. J. M. Lloyd*
★1890	Miss L. Rice *Miss M. Jacks*	★1912	Mrs. D. R. Larcombe *Mrs. A. Sterry*	★1938	Mrs. F. S. Moody *Miss H. H. Jacobs*	1965	Miss M. Smith *Miss M. E. Bueno*	1986	Miss M. Navratilova *Miss H. Mandlikova*
★1891	Miss L. Dod *Mrs. G. W. Hillyard*	★1913	Mrs. Lambert Chambers *Mrs. R. J. McNair*	★1939	Miss A. Marble *Miss K. E. Stammers*	1966	Mrs. L. W. King *Miss M. E. Bueno*	1987	Miss M. Navratilova *Miss S. Graf*
1892	Miss L. Dod *Mrs. G. W. Hillyard*	1914	Mrs. Lambert Chambers *Mrs. D. R. Larcombe*	★1946	Miss P. Betz *Miss L. Brough*	1967	Mrs. L. W. King *Mrs. P. F. Jones*	1988	Miss S. Graf *Miss M. Navratilova*
1893	Miss L. Dod *Mrs. G. W. Hillyard*	1919	Mlle. S. Lenglen *Mrs. Lambert Chambers*	★1947	Miss M. Osborne *Miss D. Hart*	1968	Mrs. L. W. King *Miss J. A. M. Tegart*	1989	Miss S. Graf *Miss M. Navratilova*
★1894	Mrs. G. W. Hillyard *Miss E. L. Austin*	1920	Mlle. S. Lenglen *Mrs. Lambert Chambers*	1948	Miss L. Brough *Miss D. Hart*	1969	Mrs. P. F. Jones *Mrs. L. W. King*	1990	Miss M. Navratilova *Miss Z. Garrison*
★1895	Miss C. Cooper *Miss H. Jackson*	1921	Mlle. S. Lenglen *Miss E. Ryan*	1949	Miss L. Brough *Mrs. W. du Pont*	★1970	Mrs. B. M. Court *Mrs. L. W. King*	1991	Miss S. Graf *Miss G. Sabatini*
1896	Miss C. Cooper *Mrs. W. H. Pickering*	†1922	Mlle. S. Lenglen *Mrs. F. Mallory*	1950	Miss L. Brough *Mrs. W. du Pont*	1971	Miss E. F. Goolagong *Mrs. B. M. Court*	1992	Miss S. Graf *Miss M. Seles*
1897	Mrs. G. W. Hillyard *Miss C. Cooper*	1923	Mlle. S. Lenglen *Miss K. McKane*	1951	Miss D. Hart *Miss S. Fry*	1972	Mrs. L. W. King *Miss E. F. Goolagong*	1993	Miss S. Graf *Miss J. Novotna*
★1898	Miss C. Cooper *Miss L Martin*	1924	Miss K. McKane *Miss H. Wills*	1952	Miss M. Connolly *Miss L. Brough*	1973	Mrs. L. W. King *Miss C. M. Evert*	1994	Miss C. Martinez *Miss M. Navratilova*
1899	Mrs. G. W. Hillyard *Miss C. Cooper*	1925	Mlle. S. Lenglen *Miss J. Fry*	1953	Miss M. Connolly *Miss D. Hart*	1974	Miss C. M. Evert *Mrs. O. Morozova*	1995	Miss S. Graf *Miss A. Sanchez Vicario*
1900	Mrs. G. W. Hillyard *Miss C. Cooper*	1926	Mrs. L. A. Godfree *Sta. L. de Alvarez*	1954	Miss M. Connolly *Miss L. Brough*	1975	Mrs. L. W. King *Mrs. R. Cawley*	1996	Miss S. Graf *Miss A. Sanchez Vicario*
1901	Mrs. A. Sterry *Mrs. G. W. Hillyard*	1927	Miss H. Wills *Sta. L. de Alvarez*	★1955	Miss L. Brough *Mrs. J. G. Fleitz*	★1976	Miss C. M. Evert *Mrs. R. Cawley*	★1997	Miss M. Hingis *Miss J. Novotna*
1902	Miss M. E. Robb *Mrs. A. Sterry*	1928	Miss H. Wills *Sta. L. de Alvarez*	1956	Miss S. Fry *Miss A. Buxton*	1977	Miss S. V. Wade *Miss B. F. Stove*	1998	Miss J. Novotna *Miss N. Tauziat*
★1903	Miss D. K. Douglass *Miss E. W. Thomson*	1929	Miss H. Wills *Miss H. H. Jacobs*	★1957	Miss A. Gibson *Miss D. R. Hard*	1978	Miss M. Navratilova *Miss C. M. Evert*	1999	Miss L.A. Davenport *Miss S. Graf*
1904	Miss D. K. Douglass *Mrs. A. Sterry*	1930	Mrs. F. S. Moody *Miss E. Ryan*	1958	Miss A. Gibson *Miss A. Mortimer*	1979	Miss M. Navratilova *Mrs. J. M. Lloyd*	2000	Miss V. Williams *Miss L.A. Davenport*
1905	Miss M. Sutton *Miss D. K. Douglass*	★1931	Fraulein C. Aussem *Fraulein H. Krahwinkel*					2001	Miss V. Williams *Miss J. Henin*
								2002	Miss S. Williams *Miss V. Williams*
								2003	Miss S. Williams *Miss V. Williams*

MAIDEN NAMES OF LADY CHAMPIONS *(In the tables the following have been recorded in both married and single identities)*

Mrs. R. Cawley............Miss E. F. Goolagong	Mrs. G. W. Hillyard............Miss B. Bingley	Mrs. L. E. G. Price ....Miss S. Reynolds	
Mrs. Lambert Chambers ....Miss D. K. Douglass	Mrs. P. F. Jones ....Miss A. S. Haydon	Mrs. G. E. Reid............Miss K. Melville	
Mrs. B. M. Court ....Miss M. Smith	Mrs. L. W. King............Miss B. J. Moffitt	Mrs. P. D. Smylie ....Miss E. M. Sayers	
Mrs. B. C. Covell............Miss P. L. Howkins	Mrs. M. R. King............Miss P. E. Mudford	Frau. S. Sperling............Fraulein H. Krahwinkel	
Mrs. D. E. Dalton............Miss J. A. M. Tegart	Mrs. D. R. Larcombe ....Miss E. W. Thomson	Mrs. A. Sterry ....Miss C. Cooper	
Mrs. W. du Pont............Miss M. Osborne	Mrs. J. M. Lloyd ....Miss C. M. Evert	Mrs. J. R. Susman ....Miss K. Hantze	
Mrs. L. A. Godfree ....Miss K. McKane	Mrs. F. S. Moody............Miss H. Wills		
Mrs. H. F. Gourlay Cawley ....Miss H. F. Gourlay	Mrs. O. Morozova............Miss O. Morozova		

GENTLEMEN'S DOUBLES

1879	L. R. Erskine and H. F. Lawford	*F. Durant and G. E. Tabor*
1880	W. Renshaw and E. Renshaw	*O. E. Woodhouse and C. J. Cole*
1881	W. Renshaw and E. Renshaw	*W. J. Down and H. Vaughan*
1882	J. T. Hartley and R. T. Richardson	*J. G. Horn and C. B. Russell*
1883	C. W. Grinstead and C. E. Welldon	*C. B. Russell and R. T. Milford*
1884	W. Renshaw and E. Renshaw	*E. W. Lewis and E. L Williams*
1885	W. Renshaw and E. Renshaw	*C. E. Farrer and A. J. Stanley*
1886	W. Renshaw and E. Renshaw	*C. E. Farrer and A. J. Stanley*
1887	P. Bowes-Lyon and H. W. W.Wilberforce	*J. H. Crispe and E. Barratt Smith*
1888	W. Renshaw and E. Renshaw	*P Bowes-Lyon and H. W. W. Wilberforce*
1889	W. Renshaw and E. Renshaw	*E. W. Lewis and G. W. Hillyard*
1890	J. Pim and F. O. Stoker	*E. W. Lewis and G. W. Hillyard*
1891	W. Baddeley and H. Baddeley	*J. Pim and F. O. Stoker*
1892	H. S. Barlow and E. W. Lewis	*W. Baddeley and H. Baddeley*
1893	J. Pim and F. O. Stoker	*E. W. Lewis and H. S. Barlow*
1894	W. Baddeley and H. Baddeley	*H. S. Barlow and C. H. Martin*
1895	W. Baddeley and H. Baddeley	*E. W. Lewis and W. V. Eaves*
1896	W. Baddeley and H. Baddeley	*R. F. Doherty and H. A. Nisbet*
1897	R. F. Doherty and H. L. Doherty	*W. Baddeley and H. Baddeley*
1898	R. F. Doherty and H. L . Doherty	*H. A. Nisbet and C. Hobart*
1899	R. F. Doherty and H. L. Doherty	*H. A. Nisbet and C. Hobart*
1900	R. F. Doherty and H. L. Doherty	*H. Roper Barrett and H. A. Nisbet*
1901	R. F. Doherty and H. L. Doherty	*Dwight Davis and Holcombe Ward*
1902	S. H. Smith and F. L. Riseley	*R. F. Doherty and H. L. Doherty*
1903	R. F. Doherty and H. L. Doherty	*S. H. Smith and F. L. Riseley*
1904	R. F. Doherty and H. L. Doherty	*S. H. Smith and F. L. Riseley*
1905	R. F. Doherty and H. L. Doherty	*S. H. Smith and F. L. Riseley*
1906	S. H. Smith and F. L. Riseley	*R. F. Doherty and H. L. Doherty*
1907	N. E. Brookes and A. F. Wilding	*B. C. Wright and K. H. Behr*
1908	A. F. Wilding and M. J. G. Ritchie	*A. W. Gore and H. Roper Barrett*
1909	A. W. Gore and H. Roper Barrett	*S. N. Doust and H. A. Parker*
1910	A. F. Wilding and M. J. G. Ritchie	*A. W. Gore and H. Roper Barrett*
1911	M. Decugis and A. H. Gobert	*M. J. G. Ritchie and A. F. Wilding*
1912	H. Roper Barrett and C. P. Dixon	*M. Decugis and A. H. Gobert*
1913	H. Roper Barrett and C. P. Dixon	*F. W. Rahe and H. Kleinschroth*
1914	N. E. Brookes and A. F. Wilding	*H. Roper Barrett and C. P. Dixon*
1919	R. V. Thomas and P. O'Hara-Wood	*R. Lycett and R. W. Heath*
1920	R. N. Williams and C. S. Garland	*A. R. F. Kingscote and J. C. Parke*
1921	R. Lycett and M. Woosnam	*F. G. Lowe and A. H. Lowe*
1922	R. Lycett and J. O. Anderson	*G. L. Patterson and P. O'Hara-Wood*
1923	R. Lycett and L. A. Godfree	*Count de Gomar and E. Flaquer*
1924	F. T. Hunter and V. Richards	*R. N. Williams and W. M. Washburn*
1925	J. Borotra and R. Lacoste	*J. Hennessey and R. Casey*
1926	H. Cochet and J. Brugnon	*V. Richards and H. Kinsey*
1927	F. T. Hunter and W. T. Tilden	*J. Brugnon and H. Cochet*
1928	H. Cochet and J. Brugnon	*G. L. Patterson and J. B. Hawkes*
1929	W. Allison and J. Van Ryn	*J. C. Gregory and I. G. Collins*
1930	W. Allison and J. Van Ryn	*J. H. Doeg and G. M. Lott*
1931	G. M Lott and J. Van Ryn	*H. Cochet and J. Brugnon*
1932	J. Borotra and J. Brugnon	*G. P. Hughes and F. J. Perry*
1933	J. Borotra and J. Brugnon	*R. Nunoi and J. Satoh*
1934	G. M. Lott and L. R. Stoefen	*J. Borotra and J. Brugnon*
1935	J. H. Crawford and A. K. Quist	*W. Allison and J. Van Ryn*
1936	G. P. Hughes and C. R. D. Tuckey	*C. E. Hare and F. H. D. Wilde*
1937	J. D. Budge and G. Mako	*G. P. Hughes and C. R. D. Tuckey*
1938	J. D. Budge and G. Mako	*H. Henkel and G. von Metaxa*
1939	R. L. Riggs and E. T. Cooke	*C. E. Hare and F. H. D. Wilde*
1946	T. Brown and J. Kramer	*G. E. Brown and D. Pails*
1947	R. Falkenburg and J. Kramer	*A. J. Mottram and O. W. Sidwell*
1948	J. E. Bromwich and F. A. Sedgman	*T. Brown and G. Mulloy*
1949	R. Gonzales and F. Parker	*G. Mulloy and F. R. Schroeder*
1950	J. E. Bromwich and A. K. Quist	*G. E. Brown and O. W Sidwell*
1951	K. McGregor and F. A. Sedgman	*J. Drobny and E. W. Sturgess*
1952	K. McGregor and F. A. Sedgman	*V. Seixas and E. W. Sturgess*
1953	L. A. Hoad and K. R. Rosewall	*R. N. Hartwig and M. G. Rose*
1954	R. N. Hartwig and M. G. Rose	*V. Seixas and T. Trabert*
1955	R. N. Hartwig and L. A. Hoad	*N. A. Fraser and K. R. Rosewall*
1956	L. A. Hoad and K. R. Rosewall	*N. Pietrangeli and O. Sirola*
1957	G. Mulloy and B. Patty	*N. A. Fraser and L. A. Hoad*
1958	S. Davidson and U. Schmidt	*A. J. Cooper and N. A. Fraser*
1959	R. Emerson and N. A. Fraser	*R. Laver and R. Mark*
1960	R. H. Osuna and R. D. Ralston	*M. G. Davies and R. K. Wilson*
1961	R. Emerson and N. A. Fraser	*R. A. J. Hewitt and F. S. Stolle*
1962	R. A. J. Hewitt and F. S. Stolle	*B. Jovanovic and N. Pilic*
1963	R. H. Osuna and A. Palafox	*J. C. Barclay and P. Darmon*
1964	R. A. J. Hewitt and F. S. Stolle	*R. Emerson and K. N. Fletcher*
1965	J. D. Newcombe and A. D. Roche	*K. N. Fletcher and R. A. J. Hewitt*
1966	K. N. Fletcher and J. D. Newcombe	*W. W. Bowrey and O. K. Davidson*
1967	R. A. J. Hewitt and F. D. McMillan	*R. Emerson and K. N. Fletcher*
1968	J. D. Newcombe and A. D. Roche	*K. R. Rosewall and F. S. Stolle*
1969	J. D. Newcombe and A. D. Roche	*T. S. Okker and M. C. Reissen*
1970	J. D. Newcombe and A. D. Roche	*K. R. Rosewall and F. S. Stolle*
1971	R. S. Emerson and R. G. Laver	*A. R. Ashe and R. D. Ralston*
1972	R. A. J. Hewitt and F. D. McMillan	*S. R. Smith and E. J. van Dillen*
1973	J. S. Connors and I. Nastase	*J. R. Cooper and N. A. Fraser*
1974	J. D. Newcombe and A. D. Roche	*R. C. Lutz and S. R. Smith*
1975	V. Gerulaitis and A. Mayer	*C. Dowdeswell and A. J. Stone*
1976	B. E. Gottfried and R. Ramirez	*R. L. Case and G. Masters*
1977	R. L. Case and G. Masters	*J. G. Alexander and P. C. Dent*
1978	R. A. J. Hewitt and F. D. McMillan	*P. Fleming and J. P. McEnroe*
1979	P. Fleming and J. P . McEnroe	*B. E. Gottfried and R. Ramirez*
1980	P. McNamara and P. McNamee	*R. C. Lutz and S. R. Smith*
1981	P. Fleming and J. P. McEnroe	*R. C. Lutz and S. R. Smith*
1982	P. McNamara and P. McNamee	*P. Fleming and J. P. McEnroe*
1983	P. Fleming and J. P McEnroe	*T. E. Gullikson and T. R. Gullikson*
1984	P. Fleming and J. P. McEnroe	*P. Cash and P. McNamee*
1985	H. P. Guenthardt and B. Taroczy	*P. Cash and J. B. Fitzgerald*
1986	J. Nystrom and M. Wilander	*G. Donnelly and P. Fleming*
1987	K. Flach and R. Seguso	*S. Casal and E. Sanchez*
1988	K. Flach and R. Seguso	*J. B. Fitzgerald and A. Jarryd*
1989	J. B. Fitzgerald and A. Jarryd	*R. Leach and J. Pugh*
1990	R. Leach and J. Pugh	*P. Aldrich and D. T. Visser*
1991	J. B. Fitzgerald and A. Jarryd	*J. Frana and L. Lavalle*
1992	J. P. McEnroe and M. Stich	*J. Grabb and R. A. Reneberg*
1993	T. A. Woodbridge and M. Woodforde	*G. Connell and P. Galbraith*
1994	T. A. Woodbridge and M. Woodforde	*G. Connell and P. Galbraith*
1995	T. A. Woodbridge and M. Woodforde	*R. Leach and S. Melville*
1996	T. A. Woodbridge and M. Woodforde	*B. Black and G. Connell*
1997	T. A. Woodbridge and M. Woodforde	*J. Eltingh and P. Haarhuis*
1998	J. Eltingh and P. Haarhuis	*T. A. Woodbridge and M. Woodforde*
1999	M. Bhupathi and L. Paes	*P. Haarhuis and J. Palmer*
2000	T. A. Woodbridge and M. Woodforde	*P. Haarhuis and S. Stolle*
2001	D. Johnson and J. Palmer	*J. Novak and D. Rikl*
2002	J. Bjorkman and T. A Woodbridge	*M. Knowles and D. Nestor*
2003	J. Bjorkman and T. A Woodbridge	*M. Bhupathi and M. Mirnyi*

LADIES' DOUBLES

1913	Mrs. R. J. McNair and Miss D. P. Boothby	*Mrs. A. Sterry and Mrs. Lambert Chambers*
1914	Miss E. Ryan and Miss A. M. Morton	*Mrs. D. R. Larcombe and Mrs. F. J. Hannam*
1919	Mlle. S. Lenglen and Miss E. Ryan	*Mrs. Lambert Chambers and Mrs. D. R. Larcombe*
1920	Mlle. S. Lenglen and Miss E. Ryan	*Mrs. Lambert Chambers and Mrs. D. R. Larcombe*
1921	Mlle. S. Lenglen and Miss E. Ryan	*Mrs. A. E. Beamish and Mrs. G. E. Peacock*
1922	Mlle. S. Lenglen and Miss E. Ryan	*Mrs. A. D. Stocks and Miss K. McKane*
1923	Mlle. S. Lenglen and Miss E. Ryan	*Miss J. Austin and Miss E. L. Colyer*
1924	Mrs. H. Wightman and Miss H. Wills	*Mrs. B. C. Covell and Miss K. McKane*
1925	Mlle. S. Lenglen and Miss E. Ryan	*Mrs. A. V. Bridge and Mrs. C. G. McIlquham*
1926	Miss E. Ryan and Miss M. K. Browne	*Mrs. L. A. Godfree and Miss E. L. Colyer*
1927	Miss H. Wills and Miss E. Ryan	*Miss E. L. Heine and Mrs. G. E. Peacock*
1928	Mrs. Holcroft-Watson and Miss P. Saunders	*Miss E. H. Harvey and Miss E. Bennett*
1929	Mrs. Holcroft-Watson and Mrs. L.R.C. Michell	*Mrs. B. C. Covell and Mrs. D. C. Shepherd-Barron*
1930	Mrs. F. S. Moody and Miss E. Ryan	*Miss E. Cross and Miss S. Palfrey*
1931	Mrs.D.C. Shepherd-Barron and MissP.E. Mudford	*Mlle. D. Metaxa and Mlle. J. Sigart*
1932	Mlle. D. Metaxa and Mlle. J. Sigart	*Miss E. Ryan and Miss H. H. Jacobs*
1933	Mme. R. Mathieu and Miss E. Ryan	*Miss F. James and Miss A. M. Yorke*
1934	Mme. R. Mathieu and Miss E. Ryan	*Mrs. D. Andrus and Mme. S. Henrotin*
1935	Miss F. James and Miss K. E. Stammers	*Mme. R. Mathieu and Frau. S. Sperling*
1936	Miss F. James and Miss K. E. Stammers	*Mrs. S. P. Fabyan and Miss H. H. Jacobs*
1937	Mme. R. Mathieu and Miss A. M. Yorke	*Mrs. M. R. King and Mrs. J. B. Pittman*
1938	Mrs. S. P. Fabyan and Miss A. Marble	*Mme. R. Mathieu and Miss A. M. Yorke*
1939	Mrs S. P. Fabyan and Miss A. Marble	*Miss H. H. Jacobs and Miss A. M. Yorke*
1946	Miss L. Brough and Miss M. Osborne	*Miss P. Betz and Miss D. Hart*
1947	Miss D. Hart and Mrs. P. C. Todd	*Miss L. Brough and Miss M. Osborne*
1948	Miss L. Brough and Mrs. W. du Pont	*Miss D. Hart and Mrs. P. C. Todd*
1949	Miss L. Brough and Mrs. W. du Pont	*Miss G. Moran and Mrs. P. C. Todd*
1950	Miss L. Brough and Mrs. W. du Pont	*Miss S. Fry and Miss D. Hart*
1951	Miss S. Fry and Miss D. Hart	*Miss L. Brough and Mrs. W. du Pont*
1952	Miss S. Fry and Miss D. Hart	*Miss L. Brough and Miss M. Connolly*
1953	Miss S. Fry and Miss D. Hart	*Miss M. Connolly and Miss J. Sampson*
1954	Miss L. Brough and Mrs. W. du Pont	*Miss S. Fry and Miss D. Hart*
1955	Miss A. Mortimer and Miss J. A. Shilcock	*Miss S. J. Bloomer and Miss P. E. Ward*
1956	Miss A. Buxton and Miss A. Gibson	*Miss F. Muller and Miss D. G. Seeney*
1957	Miss A. Gibson and Miss D. R. Hard	*Mrs. K. Hawton and Mrs. T. D. Long*
1958	Miss M. E. Bueno and Miss A. Gibson	*Mrs. W. du Pont and Miss M. Varner*
1959	Miss J. Arth and Miss D. R. Hard	*Mrs. J. G. Fleitz and Miss C. C. Truman*
1960	Miss M. E. Bueno and Miss D. R. Hard	*Miss S. Reynolds and Miss R. Schuurman*
1961	Miss K. Hantze and Miss B. J. MoYtt	*Miss J. Lehane and Miss M. Smith*
1962	Miss B. J. MoYtt and Mrs. J. R. Susman	*Mrs. L. E. G. Price and Miss R. Schuurman*
1963	Miss M. E. Bueno and Miss D. R. Hard	*Miss R. A. Ebbern and Miss M. Smith*
1964	Miss M. Smith and Miss L. R. Turner	*Miss B. J. MoYtt and Mrs. J. R. Susman*
1965	Miss M. E. Bueno and Miss B. J. MoYtt	*Miss F. Durr and Miss J. LieVrig*
1966	Miss M. E. Bueno and Miss N. Richey	*Miss M. Smith and Miss J. A. M. Tegart*
1967	Miss R. Casals and Mrs. L. W. King	*Miss M. E. Bueno and Miss N. Richey*
1968	Miss R. Casals and Mrs. L. W. King	*Miss F. Durr and Mrs. P. F. Jones*
1969	Mrs. B. M. Court and Miss J. A. M. Tegart	*Miss P. S. A. Hogan and Miss M. Michel*
1970	Miss R. Casals and Mrs. L. W. King	*Miss F. Durr and Miss S. V. Wade*
1971	Miss R. Casals and Mrs. L. W. King	*Mrs. B. M. Court and Miss E. F. Goolagong*
1972	Mrs. L. W. King and Miss B. F. Stove	*Mrs. D. E. Dalton and Miss F. Durr*
1973	Miss R. Casals and Mrs. L. W. King	*Miss F. Durr and Miss B. F. Stove*
1974	Miss E. F. Goolagong and Miss M. Michel	*Miss H. F. Gourlay and Miss K. M. Krantzcke*
1975	Miss A. Kiyomura and Miss K. Sawamatsu	*Miss F. Durr and Miss B. F. Stove*
1976	Miss C. M. Evert and Miss M. Navratilova	*Mrs. L. W. King and Miss B. F. Stove*
1977	Mrs. H. F. Gourlay Cawley and Miss J. C. Russell	*Miss M. Navratilova and Miss B. F . Stove*
1978	Mrs. G. E. Reid and Miss. W. M. Turnbull	*Miss M. Jausovec and Miss V. Ruzici*
1979	Mrs. L. W. King and Miss M. Navratilova	*Miss B. F. Stove and Miss W. M. Turnbull*
1980	Miss K. Jordan and Miss A. E. Smith	*Miss R. Casals and Miss W. M. Turnbull*
1981	Miss M. Navratilova and Miss P. H. Shriver	*Miss K. Jordan and Miss A. E. Smith*
1982	Miss M. Navratilova and Miss P. H. Shriver	*Miss K. Jordan and Miss A. E. Smith*
1983	Miss M. Navratilova and Miss P. H. Shriver	*Miss R. Casals and Miss W. M. Turnbull*
1984	Miss M. Navratilova and Miss P. H. Shriver	*Miss K. Jordan and Miss A. E. Smith*
1985	Miss K. Jordan and Mrs. P. D. Smylie	*Miss M. Navratilova and Miss P. H. Shriver*
1986	Miss M. Navratilova and Miss P. H. Shriver	*Miss H. Mandlikova and Miss W. M. Turnbull*
1987	Miss C. Kohde-Kilsch and Miss H. Sukova	*Miss B. Nagelsen and Mrs. P. D. Smylie*
1988	Miss S. Graf and Miss G. Sabatini	*Miss L. Savchenko and Miss N. Zvereva*
1989	Miss J. Novotna and Miss H. Sukova	*Miss L. Savchenko and Miss N. Zvereva*
1990	Miss J. Novotna and Miss H. Sukova	*Miss K. Jordan and Mrs. P. D. Smylie*
1991	Miss L. Savchenko and Miss N. Zvereva	*Miss G. Fernandez and Miss J. Novotna*
1992	Miss G. Fernandez and Miss N. Zvereva	*Miss J. Novotna and Mrs. L. Savchenko-Neiland*
1993	Miss G. Fernandez and Miss N. Zvereva	*Mrs. L. Neiland and Miss J. Novotna*
1994	Miss G. Fernandez and Miss N. Zvereva	*Miss J. Novotna and Miss A. Sanchez Vicario*
1995	Miss J. Novotna and Miss A. Sanchez Vicario	*Miss G. Fernandez and Miss N. Zvereva*
1996	Miss M. Hingis and Miss H. Sukova	*Miss M.J. McGrath and Mrs. L. Neiland*
1997	Miss G. Fernandez and Miss N. Zvereva	*Miss N.J. Arendt and Miss M.M. Bollegraf*
1998	Miss M. Hingis and Miss J. Novotna	*Miss L.A. Davenport and Miss N. Zvereva*
1999	Miss L.A. Davenport and Miss C. Morariu	*Miss M. de Swardt and Miss E. Tatarkova*
2000	Miss S. Williams and Miss V. Williams	*Mrs J. Halard–Decugis and Miss A. Sugiyama*
2001	Miss L.M. Raymond and Miss R.P. Stubbs	*Miss K. Clijsters and Miss A. Sugiyama*
2002	Miss S. Williams and Miss V. Williams	*Miss V. Ruano Pascual and Miss P. Suarez*
2003	Miss K. Clijsters and Miss A. Sugiyama	*Miss V. Ruano Pascual and Miss P. Suarez*

THE CHAMPIONSHIP ROLL

MIXED DOUBLES

1913 H. Crisp and Mrs. C. O. Tuckey
J. C. Parke and Mrs. D. R. Larcombe
1914 J. C. Parke and Mrs. D.R. Larcombe
A. F. Wilding and Mlle. M. Broquedis
1919 R. Lycett and Miss E. Ryan
A. D. Prebble and Mrs. Lambert Chambers
1920 G. L. Patterson and Mlle. S. Lenglen
R. Lycett and Miss E. Ryan
1921 R. Lycett and Miss E. Ryan
M. Woosnam and Miss P. L. Howkins
1922 P. O'Hara-Wood and Mlle. S. Lenglen
R. Lycett and Miss E. Ryan
1923 R. Lycett and Miss E. Ryan
L. S. Deane and Mrs. D. C. Shepherd-Barron
1924 J. B. Gilbert and Miss K. McKane
L. A. Godfree and Mrs. D. C. Shepherd-Barron
1925 J. Borotra and Mlle. S. Lenglen
H. L. de Morpurgo and Miss E. Ryan
1926 L. A. Godfree and Mrs. L. A. Godfree
H. Kinsey and Miss M. K. Browne
1927 F. T. Hunter and Miss E. Ryan
L. A. Godfree and Mrs. L. A. Godfree
1928 P. D. B. Spence and Miss E. Ryan
J. Crawford and Miss D. Akhurst
1929 F. T. Hunter and Miss H. Wills
I. G. Collins and Miss J. Fry
1930 J. H. Crawford and Miss E. Ryan
D. Prenn and Fraulein H. Krahwinkel
1931 G. M. Lott and Mrs L. A. Harper
I. G. Collins and Miss J. C. Ridley
1932 E. Maier and Miss E. Ryan
H. C. Hopman and Mlle. J. Sigart
1933 G. von Cramm and Fraulein H. Krahwinkel
N. G. Farquharson and Miss M. Heeley
1934 R. Miki and Miss D. E. Round
H. W. Austin and Mrs D. C. Shepherd-Barron
1935 F. J. Perry and Miss D. E. Round
H. C. Hopman and Mrs. H. C. Hopman
1936 F. J. Perry and Miss D. E. Round
J. D. Budge and Mrs. S. P. Fabyan
1937 J. D. Budge and Miss A. Marble

Y. Petra and Mme. R. Mathieu
1938 J. D. Budge and Miss A. Marble
H. Henkel and Mrs. S. P. Fabyan
1939 R. L. Riggs and Miss A. Marble
F. H. D. Wilde and Miss N. B. Brown
1946 T. Brown and Miss L. Brough
G. E. Brown and Miss D. Bundy
1947 J. E. Bromwich and Miss L. Brough
C. F. Long and Mrs. N. M. Bolton
1948 J. E. Bromwich and Miss L. Brough
F. A. Sedgman and Miss D. Hart
1949 E. W. Sturgess and Mrs. S. P. Summers
J. E. Bromwich and Miss L. Brough
1950 E. W. Sturgess and Miss L. Brough
G. E. Brown and Mrs. P. C. Todd
1951 F. A. Sedgman and Miss D. Hart
M. G. Rose and Mrs. N. M. Bolton
1952 F. A. Sedgman and Miss D. Hart
E. Morea and Mrs. T. D. Long
1953 V. Seixas and Miss D. Hart
E. Morea and Miss S. Fry
1954 V. Seixas and Miss D. Hart
K. R. Rosewall and Mrs. W. du Pont
1955 V. Seixas and Miss D. Hart
E. Morea and Miss L. Brough
1956 V. Seixas and Miss S. Fry
G. Mulloy and Miss A. Gibson
1957 M. G. Rose and Miss D. R. Hard
N. A. Fraser and Miss A. Gibson
1958 R. N. Howe and Miss L. Coghlan
K. Nielsen and Miss A. Gibson
1959 R. Laver and Miss D. R. Hard
N. A. Fraser and Miss M. E. Bueno
1960 R. Laver and Miss D. R. Hard
R. N. Howe and Miss M. E. Bueno
1961 F. S. Stolle and Miss L. R. Turner
R. N. Howe and Miss E. Buding
1962 N. A. Fraser and Mrs. W. du Pont
R. D. Ralston and Miss A. S. Haydon
1963 K. N. Fletcher and Miss M. Smith
R. A. J. Hewitt and Miss D. R. Hard

1964 F. S. Stolle and Miss L. R. Turner
K. N. Fletcher and Miss M. Smith
1965 K. N. Fletcher and Miss M. Smith
A. D. Roche and Miss J. A. M. Tegart
1966 K. N. Fletcher and Miss M. Smith
R. D. Ralston and Mrs. L. W. King
1967 O. K. Davidson and Mrs. L. W. King
K. N. Fletcher and Miss M. E. Bueno
1968 K. N. Fletcher and Mrs. B. M. Court
A. Metreveli and Miss O. Morozova
1969 F. S. Stolle and Mrs. P. F. Jones
A. D. Roche and Mrs. J. A. M. Tegart
1970 I. Nastase and Miss R. Casals
A. Metreveli and Miss O. Morozova
1971 O. K. Davidson and Mrs. L. W. King
M. C. Riessen and Mrs. B. M. Court
1972 I. Nastase and Miss R. Casals
K.G. Warwick and Miss E. F. Goolagong
1973 O. K. Davidson and Mrs. L. W. King
R. Ramirez and Miss J. S. Newberry
1974 O. K. Davidson and Mrs. L. W. King
M. J. Farrell and Miss L. J. Charles
1975 M. C. Riessen and Mrs. B. M. Court
A. J. Stone and Miss G. F. Stove
1976 A. D. Roche and Miss F. Durr
R. L. Stockton and Miss R. Casals
1977 R. A. J. Hewitt and Miss G. R. Stevens
F. D. McMillan and Miss B. F. Stove
1978 F. D. McMillan and Miss B. F. Stove
R. O. Ruffels and Mrs. L. W. King
1979 R. A. J. Hewitt and Miss G. R. Stevens
F. D. McMillan and Miss B. F. Stove
1980 J. R. Austin and Miss T. Austin
M. R. Edmondson and Miss D. L. Fromholtz
1981 F. D. McMillan and Miss B. F. Stove
J. R. Austin and Miss T. Austin
1982 K. Curren and Miss A. E. Smith
J. M. Lloyd and Miss W. M. Turnbull
1983 J. M. Lloyd and Miss W. M. Turnbull
S. Denton and Mrs. L. W. King
1984 J. M. Lloyd and Miss W. M. Turnbull

S. Denton and Miss K. Jordan
1985 P. McNamee and Miss M. Navratilova
J. B. Fitzgerald and Mrs. P. D. Smylie
1986 K. Flach and Miss K. Jordan
H. P. Guenthardt and Miss M. Navratilova
1987 M. J. Bates and Miss J. M. Durie
D. Cahill and Miss N. Provis
1988 S. E. Stewart and Miss Z. L. Garrison
K. Jones and Mrs. S. W. Magers
1989 J. Pugh and Miss J. Novotna
M. Kratzmann and Miss J. M. Byrne
1990 R. Leach and Miss Z. L. Garrison
J. B. Fitzgerald and Mrs P. D. Smylie
1991 J. B. Fitzgerald and Miss P. D. Smylie
J. Pugh and Miss N. Zvereva
1992 C. Suk and Miss L. Savchenko-Neiland
J. Eltingh and Miss M. Oremans
1993 M. Woodforde and Miss M. Navratilova
T. Nijssen and Miss M. M. Bollegraf
1994 T. A. Woodbridge and Miss H. Sukova
T. J. Middleton and Miss L. M. McNeil
1995 J. Stark and Miss M. Navratilova
C. Suk and Miss G. Fernandez
1996 C. Suk and Miss H. Sukova
M. Woodforde and Mrs. L. Neiland
1997 C. Suk and Miss H. Sukova
A. Olhovskiy and Miss L. Neiland
1998 M. Mirnyi and Miss S. Williams
M. Bhupathi and Miss M. Lucic
1999 L. Paes and Miss L.M. Raymond
J. Bjorkman and Miss A. Kournikova
2000 D. Johnson and Miss K. Po
L. Hewitt and Miss K. Clijsters
2001 L. Friedl and Miss D. Hantuchova
M. Bryan and Mrs L. Huber
2002 M. Bhupathi and Miss E. Likhovtseva
K. Ullyett and Miss D. Hantuchova
2003 L. Paes and Miss M. Navratilova
A. Ram and Miss A. Rodionova

THE JUNIOR CHAMPIONSHIP ROLL

BOYS' SINGLES

1947 K. Nielsen (Denmark)
S. V. Davidson (Sweden)
1948 S. Stockenberg (Sweden)
D. Vad (Hungary)
1949 S. Stockenberg (Sweden)
J. A. T. Horn (G.B.)
1950 J. A.T. Horn (G.B.)
K. Mobarek (Egypt)
1951 J. Kupferburger (S.A.)
K. Mobarek (Egypt)
1952 R. K. Wilson (G.B.)
T. T. Fancutt (S.A.)
1953 W. A. Knight (G.B.)
R. Krishnan (India)
1954 R. Krishnan (India)
A. J. Cooper (Australia)
1955 M. P. Hann (G.B.)
J. E. Lundquist (Sweden)
1956 R. Holmberg (U.S.A.)

R. G. Laver (Australia)
1957 J. I. Tattersall (G.B.)
I. Ribeiro (Brazil)
1958 E. Buchholz (U.S.A.)
P. J. Lall (India)
1959 T. Lejus (U.S.S.R.)
R. W. Barnes (Brazil)
1960 A. R. Mandelstam (S.A.)
J. Mukerjea (India)
1961 C. E. Graebner (U.S.A.)
E. Blanke (Austria)
1962 S. Matthews (G.B.)
A. Metreveli (U.S.S.R.)
1963 N. Kalogeropoulos (Greece)
I. El Shafei (U.A.R.)
1964 I. El Shafei (U.A.R.)
V. Korotkov (U.S.S.R.)
1965 V. Korotkov (u.s.s.r.)
G. Goven (France)

1966 V. Korotkov (U.S.S.R.)
B. E. Fairlie (N.Z.)
1967 M. Orantes (Spain)
M. S. Estep (U.S.A.)
1968 J. G. Alexander (Australia)
J. Thamin (France)
1969 B. Bertram (S.A.)
J. G. Alexander (Australia)
1970 B. Bertram (S.A.)
F. Gebert (Germany)
1971 R. Kreiss (U.S.A.)
S. A. Warboys (G.B.)
1972 B. Borg (Sweden)
C. J. Mottram (G.B.)
1973 W. Martin (U.S.A.)
C. S. Dowdeswell (Rhodesia)
1974 *Ash Amritraj (India)*
1975 C. J. Lewis (N.Z.)

1976 R. Ycaza (Ecuador)
H. Guenthardt (Switzerland)
1977 P. Elter (Germany)
V. A. Winitsky (U.S.A.)
1978 T. E. Teltscher (U.S.A.)
I. Lendl (Czechoslovakia)
1979 J. Turpin (U.S.A.)
R. Krishnan (India)
1980 D. Siegler (U.S.A.)
T. Tulasne (France)
1981 H. D. Beutel (Germany)
M. W. Anger (U.S.A.)
1982 P. Cash (Australia)
H. Sundstrom (Sweden)
1983 S. Edberg (Sweden)
J. Frawley (Australia)
1984 M.Kratzmann (Australia)
S. Kruger (S.A.)

1985 L. Lavalle (Mexico)
E. Velez (Mexico)
1986 E. Velez (Mexico)
J. Sanchez (Spain)
1987 D. Nargiso (Italy)
J. R. Stoltenberg (Australia)
1988 N. Pereira (Venezuela)
G. Raoux (France)
1989 N. Kulti (Sweden)
T. A. Woodbridge (Australia)
1990 L. Paes (India)
M. Ondruska (S.A.)
1991 T. Enquist (Sweden)
M. Joyce (U.S.A.)
1992 S. Skoch (Czechoslovakia)
B. Dunn (U.S.A.)
1993 R. Sabau (Romania)
J. Szymanski (Venezuela)
1994 S. Humphries (U.S.A.)

M. A. Philippoussis (Australia)
1995 O. Mutis (France)
N. Kiefer (Germany)
1996 V. Voltchkov (Belarus)
I. Ljubicic (Croatia)
1997 W. Whitehouse (South Africa)
D. Elsner (Germany)
1998 R. Federer (Switzerland)
I. Labadze (Georgia)
1999 J. Melzer (Austria)
K. Pless (Denmark)
2000 N. Mahut (France)
M. Ancic (Croatia)
2001 R. Valent (Switzerland)
G. Muller (Luxembourg)
2002 T. Reid (Australia)
L. Quahab (Algeria)
2003 F. Mergea (Romania)
C. Guccione (Australia)

BOYS' DOUBLES

1982 P. Cash and J. Frawley
R. D. Leach and J. J. Ross
1983 M. Kratzmann and S. Youl
M. Nastase and O. Rahnasto
1984 R. Brown and R. Weiss
M. Kratzmann and J. Svensson
1985 A. Moreno and J. Yzaga
P. Korda and C. Suk
1986 T. Carbonell and P. Korda

S. Barr and H. Karrasch
1987 J-L. De Jager and T. Woodbridge
D. Nargiso and E. Rossi
1988 J. Stoltenberg and T. Woodbridge
D. Rikl and T. Zdrazila
1989 J. Palmer and J. Stark
J-L. De Jager and W. R. Ferreira
1990 S. Lareau and S. Leblanc
C. Marsh and M. Ondruska

1991 K. Alami and G. Rusedski
J-L. De Jager and A. Medvedev
1992 S. Baldas and S. Draper
M. S. Bhupathi and N. Kirtane
1993 S. Downs and J. Greenhalgh
N. Godwin and G. Williams
1994 B. Ellwood and M. Philippoussis
V. Platenik and R. Schlachter
1995 M. Lee and J.M. Trotman

A. Hernandez and M. Puerta
1996 D. Bracciali and J. Robichaud
D. Roberts and W. Whitehouse
1997 L. Horna and N. Massu
J. Van de Westhuizen and W. Whitehouse
1998 R. Federer and O. Rochus
M. Llodra and A. Ram
1999 G. Coria and D. Nalbandian
T. Enev and J. Nieminem

2000 D. Coene and K. Vliegen
A. Banks and B. Riby
2001 F. Dancevic and G. Lapentti
B. Echagaray and S. Gonzales
2002 F. Mergea and H. Tecau
B. Baker and B. Ram
2003 F. Mergea and H. Tecau
A. Feeney and C. Guccione

GIRLS' SINGLES

1947 Miss G. Domken (Belgium)
Miss B. Wallen (Sweden)
1948 Miss O. Miskova (Czechoslovakia)
Miss V. Rigollet (Switzerland)
1949 Miss C. Mercelis (Belgium)
Miss J. S. V. Partridge (G.B.)
1950 Miss L. Cornell (G.B.)
Miss A. Winter (Norway)
1951 Miss L. Cornell (G.B.)
Miss S. Lazzarino (Italy)
1952 Miss F. J. I. ten Bosch (Netherlands)
Miss R. Davar (India)
1953 Miss D. Kilian (S.A.)
Miss V. A. Pitt (G.B.)
1954 Miss V. A. Pitt (G.B.)
Miss C. Monnot (France)
1955 Miss S. M. Armstrong (G.B.)
Miss B. de Chambure (France)
1956 Miss A. S. Haydon (G.B.)
Miss I. Buding (Germany)
1957 Miss M. Arnold (U.S.A.)
Miss E. Reyes (Mexico)
1958 Miss S. M. Moore (U.S.A.)

Miss A. Dmitrieva (U.S.S.R.)
1959 Miss J. Cross (S.A.)
Miss D. Schuster (Austria)
1960 Miss K. Hantze (U.S.A.)
Miss L. M Hutchings (S.A.)
1961 Miss G. Baksheeva (U.S.S.R.)
Miss K. D. Chabot (U.S.A.)
1962 Miss G. Baksheeva (U.S.S.R.)
Miss E. P. Terry (N.Z.)
1963 Miss D. M. Salfati (France)
Miss M. Dening (Australia)
1964 Miss P. Bartkowicz (U.S.A.)
Miss E. Subirats (Mexico)
1965 Miss O. Morozova (U.S.S.R.)
Miss R. Giscarfe (Argentina)
1966 Miss B. Lindstrom (Finland)
Miss J. A. Congdon (G.B.)
1967 Miss J. Salome (Netherlands)
Miss E. M. Strandberg (Sweden)
1968 Miss K. Pigeon (U.S.A.)
Miss L. E. Hunt (Australia)
1969 Miss K. Sawamatsu (Japan)
Miss B. I. Kirk (S.A.)

1970 Miss S. Walsh (U.S.A.)
Miss M.V. Kroshina (U.S.S.R.)
1971 Miss M.V. Kroshina (U.S.S.R.)
Miss S. H. Minford (G.B.)
1972 Miss I. Kloss (S.A.)
Miss G. L. Coles (G.B.)
1973 Miss A. Kiyomura (U.S.A.)
Miss M. Navratilova (Czechoslovakia)
1974 Miss M. Jausovec (Yugoslavia)
Miss M. Simionescu (Romania)
1975 Miss N. Y. Chmyreva (U.S.S.R.)
Miss R. Marsikova (Czechoslovakia)
1976 Miss N. Y. Chmyreva (U.S.S.R.)
Miss M. Kruger (S.A.)
1977 Miss L. Antonoplis (U.S.A.)
Miss Mareen Louie (U.S.A.)
1978 Miss T. Austin (U.S.A.)
Miss H. Mandlikova (Czechoslovakia)
1979 Miss M. L. Piatek (U.S.A.)
Miss A. A. Moulton (U.S.A.)
1980 Miss D. Freeman (Australia)
Miss S. J. Leo (Australia)
1981 Miss Z. Garrison (U.S.A.)

1982 Miss R. R. Uys (S.A.)
Miss C. Tanvier (France)
1983 Miss H. Sukova (Czechoslovakia)
Miss P. Paradis (France)
1984 Miss A. N. Croft (G.B.)
Miss E. Reinach (S.A.)
1985 Miss A. Holikova (Czechoslovakia)
Miss J. M. Byrne (Australia)
1986 Miss N.M. Zvereva (U.S.S.R.)
Miss L. Meskhi (U.S.S.R.)
1987 Miss N.M. Zvereva (U.S.S.R.)
Miss J. Halard (France)
1988 Miss B. Schultz (Netherlands)
Miss E. Derly (France)
1989 Miss A. Strnadova (Czechoslovakia)
Miss M. J. McGrath (U.S.A.)
1990 Miss A. Strnadova (Czechoslovakia)
Miss K. Sharpe (Australia)
1991 Miss B. Rittner (Germany)
Miss E. Makarova (U.S.A.)
1992 Miss C. Rubin (U.S.A.)
Miss L. Courtois (Belgium)

1993 Miss N. Feber (Belgium)
Miss R. Grande (Italy)
1994 Miss M. Hingis (Switzerland)
Miss M-R. Jeon (Korea)
1995 Miss A. Olsza (Poland)
Miss T. Tanasugarn (Thailand)
1996 Miss A. Mauresmo (France)
Miss M. L. Serna (Spain)
1997 Miss C. Black (Zimbabwe)
Miss A. Rippner (U.S.A.)
1998 Miss K. Srebotnik (Slovenia)
Miss K. Clijsters (Belgium)
1999 Miss I. Tulyagnova (Uzbekistan)
Miss L. Krasnoroutskaya (U.S.S.R.)
2000 Miss M. E. Salerni (Argentina)
Miss T. Perebiynis (Ukraine)
2001 Miss A. Widjaja (Indonesia)
Miss D. Safina (U.S.S.R.)
2002 Miss V. Douchevina (Russia)
Miss M. Sharapova (U.S.S.R.)
2003 Miss K. Flipkens (Belgium)
Miss A. Tchakvetadze (U.S.S.R.)

GIRLS' DOUBLES

1982 Miss B. Herr and Miss P. Barg
Miss B. S. Gerken and Miss G. A. Rush
1983 Miss P. Fendick and Miss P. Hy
Miss C. Anderholm and Miss H. Olsson
1984 Miss C. Kuhlman and Miss S. Rehe
Miss V. Milvidskaya and Miss L. I. Savchenko
1985 Miss L. Field and Miss J. Thompson
Miss E. Reinach and Miss J. A. Richardson
1986 Miss M. Jaggard and Miss L. O'Neill
Miss L. Meskhi and Miss N. M. Zvereva
1987 Miss N. Medvedeva and Miss N.M. Zvereva

Miss I. S. Kim and Miss P. M. Moreno
1988 Miss J. A. Faull and Miss R. McQuillan
Miss A. Dechaume and Miss E. Derly
1989 Miss J. Capriati and Miss M. McGrath
Miss A. Strnadova and Miss A. Strnadova
1990 Miss K. Habsudova and Miss A. Strnadova
Miss N. J. Pratt and Miss K. Sharpe
1991 Miss C. Barclay and Miss L. Zaltz
Miss J. Limmer and Miss A. Woolcock
1992 Miss M. Avotins and Miss L. McShea
Miss P. Nelson and Miss J. Steven

1993 Miss L. Courtois and Miss N. Feber
Miss H. Mochizuki and Miss Y. Yoshida
1994 Miss E. De Villiers and Miss E. E. Jelfs
Miss C. M. Morariu and Miss L. Varmuzova
1995 Miss C. Black and Miss A. Olsza
Miss T. Musgrove and Miss J Richardson
1996 Miss O. Barabanschikova and Miss A. Mauresmo
Miss L. Osterloh and Miss S. Reeves
1997 Miss C. Black and Miss I. Selyutina
Miss M. Matevzic and Miss K. Srebotnik
1998 Miss E. Dyrberg and Miss J. Kostanic

Miss P. Rampre and Miss I. Tulyagnova
1999 Miss D. Bedanova and Miss M.E. Salerni
Miss T. Perebiynis and Miss I. Tulyagnova
2000 Miss I. Gaspar and Miss T. Perebiynis
Miss D. Bedanova and Miss M. E. Salerni
2001 Miss G. Dulko and Miss A. Harkleroad
Miss C. Horiatopoulos and Miss B. Mattek
2002 Miss E. Clijsters and Miss B. Strycova
Miss A. Baker and Miss A-L. Groenfeld
2003 Miss A. Kleybanova and Miss M. Mirza
Miss K. Bohmova and Miss M. Krajicek